SEVEN WONDERS OF THE SPIRITUAL WORLD

SEVEN WONDERS OF THE SPIRITUAL WORLD

BILL HYBELS

WORD PUBLISHING
Nelson Word Ltd
Milton Keynes, England

WORD AUSTRALIA
Kilsyth, Victoria, Australia

NELSON WORD CANADA LTD
Vancouver, B.C., Canada

STRUIK CHRISTIAN BOOKS (PTY) LTD
Cape Town, South Africa

JOINT DISTRIBUTORS SINGAPORE –
ALBY COMMERCIAL ENTERPRISES PTE LTD
and
CAMPUS CRUSADE ASIA LTD

CHRISTIAN MARKETING NEW ZEALAND LTD
Havelock North, New Zealand

JENSCO LTD
Hong Kong

SALVATION BOOK CENTRE
Malaysia

SEVEN WONDERS OF THE SPIRITUAL WORLD

Copyright © 1988 by Bill Hybels.

First published in the USA by Word Incorporated, Dallas.

First UK edition 1993 by Nelson Word Ltd., Milton Keynes, England.

ISBN 0-85009-633-2   (Australia ISBN 1-86258-308-0)

Unless otherwise indicated, all Scripture quotations are from the New American Standard Bible, copyright © 1960, 1962, 1963, 1968, 1971, 1972, 1973, 1975, 1977 by the Lockman Foundation and used by permission.

Reproduced, printed and bound in Great Britain for Nelson Word Ltd. by Cox and Wyman Ltd., Reading.

93 94 95 96 / 10 9 8 7 6 5 4 3 2 1

To my wife
LYNNE
and my children
SHAUNA and TODD
the three most precious
wonders in my world

Contents

Acknowledgments

I am grateful to the congregation of Willow Creek Community Church for enduring thirteen years of my pastoring; to the elders, staff and board members whose devotion to Christ inspires me continually; to Quig and Jon and Rich who hold me accountable in private for what I say in public; to Jerry Jenkins for his assistance in preparing this manuscript; and to my spiritual mentor, Dr. Bilezikian, whose contribution to my life has been incalculable.

DO NOT
MARK IN
THIS BOOK

Introduction:

Why I Care

WE WERE ON THE WAY home from church when I was about thirteen. My father told me about one of his business associates.

"He's been going through a rough time in his marriage, so I've been talking to him about spiritual things. I think I'll invite him to church."

Reflexively, I said, "Dad! Don't bring him to church if he's just beginning to get interested in Christianity!"

I was convinced that if the man spent an hour as we just had, it would extinguish whatever flame had been lit in his life. I blurted that out without hours philosophizing on the nature or goals of the church. I just knew instinctively that our church was trouble for seekers.

A few years later I went to high school with a guy who lived on the edge of disaster. He was one of the drinkers, the fighters. We played sports together and were close for a long time. He had no interest in spiritual matters until he was jilted by his girl friend. He was so distraught that he admitted he was confused about a lot of things. He said, "I'd like to come to church with you."

I was so glad to see this wanderer finally start to take things seriously that I took him to church.

Through the whole service I cringed. I was looking at it through the eyes of a seeker, somebody who needed Christ, somebody who was investigating Christianity. When the pianist massacred the prelude, I thought, *Oh my.* I had never really listened to the prelude before; what did I care? Then a guy got up to read Scripture, some Old Testament passage that made no sense to a seeker. During the special music, I wanted to crawl under the pew.

Our pastor taught systematically through the Heidelberg Catechism. That Sunday it had little to do with life as I knew it.

With a friend sitting next to me in a posture of spiritual openness, I realized that everything in that service was either not designed for him, or was offending him.

I looked for my friend at school the next day. And the next. Finally I tracked him down.

"What's going on? We hang out together. Where've you been?"

"I always thought you were sort of normal," he said. "A regular guy. You talk regular, you dress regular, you act regular. That's why I like you. I know you're a Christian, but I want to know why you go to what you took me to Sunday. A normal person wouldn't do that. Why do you do it?"

I knew why. I was already convinced. Christianity and church was a way of life for me. I didn't get up Sunday mornings and wonder whether I was going to church. I went. My parents instilled that in me when I was just a little guy. I wasn't critical about what we were trying to accomplish, who we were trying to reach, whether we were making a difference. I went along with the program. I did what everybody was doing. Come in, sit, put your mind on autopilot until it's over, and leave.

Now here was a seeker pressing me. In effect, he was saying, "What is going on? Why do those people do what they do? Who are they doing it for? They weren't doing it for me." He was asking a second question, equally troublesome. "What are they doing for you? Is that the kind of thing you like? Does it build you up? Is it meaningful to you?"

He never came back. To this day he is not walking with the Lord.

Those two incidents proved foundational in my philosophical journey toward what the church is all about—as a junior high kid, reflexively telling my dad not to take a seeker to church, and then as a high schooler, taking a seeker to church and getting burned.

After planning to go into business and spending a couple of years in college studying economics and business administration, I felt distinctly called of God to leave the marketplace. I discuss this further in chapter three, but for now let me tell you about my first year in part-time ministry, as a twenty-year-old.

South Park Church, in Park Ridge, Illinois, had just lost its youth pastor. A friend of mine led the music ministry for the little youth group, and he asked me to try to feed the kids spiritually. He suggested I put together some devotionals, open the Bible, and teach about twenty-five kids. I said I would try.

It surprised me, but when I taught from the Bible, kids listened. Where I grew up, we never took a youth sponsor seriously. We went through them annually, chewing them up and spitting them out. Now here I was, opening the Bible and talking, and I could see in the eyes of the young people that they were listening, and learning, and growing.

In my personal Bible study I had discovered what spiritual gifts were. I wondered, *Could it be that God has given me the gift of teaching?*

The more I taught and opened the Word, and the more those kids grew and developed spiritually, the more astounded I was by the realization that God had chosen me—a sinner, saved by His grace —to teach His Word. He had instilled in me a gift I didn't deserve, that I never asked for. When I discovered this, in my own spirit I decided that if I accomplished nothing else in my life, it was enough to take and stretch my gift. I wanted to develop it and present it back to God.

I took the teaching assignment seriously, spending time in preparation and agonizing over messages for those kids. The effect was amazing. Those students, somewhat disenfranchised and uninterested when I first came, began growing in their love for Christ and for one another.

When other kids from the church who had never participated in the youth group started joining, the twenty-five became thirty-five, then forty-five, then fifty-five. I thought, *This is unbelievable.*

After many months of intense Bible study, I thought we ought to learn what the word said about reaching out, and then we ought to do it. I taught a couple of lessons on evangelism, about not just talking about reaching lost high school students for Christ, but really doing it. The kids resonated with it. At prayer meetings in the basement of the church, kids prayed for their lost, wayward high school friends. One night I said, "Here's the plan. In a couple of weeks, let's each think of one or two students we've been praying for, and let's bring them here. We'll try to lead them to Christ and teach them the Word."

One of the students said, "We have a problem with your plan."

I was taken aback, but something within me—I now know it was the Holy Spirit—urged me to stop and listen. The student continued, "I wouldn't want to bring one of my unsaved friends to this youth group. Look where we're meeting. We're in the dark corner of the basement of a church. I'd be embarrassed."

That opened things up. Another student said, "You think *where* we're meeting is embarrassing. The music is a problem, too."

I thought we could fix those things, but then another kid said, "Bill, I want to say something about your teaching."

I swallowed hard, but I listened.

"When you teach, you spend forty-five minutes going all over the Bible, and you go from one subject to another. We know where these Scriptures are, and we don't mind you taking *us* on long journeys in and around interesting places. But, I don't think my nonchurched friends are going to hang with you."

I said, "How would you do it?" The collective wisdom from that meeting went like this:

Choose one subject from Scripture that really touches human life, something a high school student can identify with, something that will convince him the Bible speaks to where he lives. Illustrate it, keep it to twenty or twenty-five minutes, then challenge him to do something about it.

Someone said, "Let's have creative things at the meeting, like drama." I have to admit I didn't really know what he was talking about. But in suburban Chicago there were tremendous theater programs in the local high schools. Lots of actors and actresses put on full-scale productions. The kids said, "We could dramatize what you're talking about, make it come alive."

Someone else suggested multimedia, and a couple of kids said they could handle that. We kept brainstorming, and out of that experience came what was to be known as the Son City youth ministry concept. It was predicated on the fact that a seeker is fundamentally different in composition than someone who is already convinced and a part of the Christian family. If you're going to reach people outside the family of God, you must program and orient whatever you do toward that person.

To the already-convinced, you can spend forty-five minutes in exaltation, singing, reading, praying, and having communion. The already-convinced want that. They have an appetite for it. They want to plumb the depths of the mysteries of God. They want to participate in worship and exaltation.

The seeker is fundamentally different.

The lesson taught me by those high school students brought me back to the junior high conversation with my dad and to the high school friend I took to church. I had to come to terms with the fact that even after those landmark experiences, I had made the same stupid mistake. By the way I was leading a Christian group, I effectively froze out the very people whom Jesus Christ said He had come to seek and to save. That was a humbling awareness.

When the youth group kids brought their friends, those friends found that the whole evening was just for them. The music was their style, except the lyrics were about Jesus Christ. Drama might split them with laughter or have them in tears. Those seeking students were thinking, *These people might be Christians, but they understand what I'm going through. And they care.*

What kind of impression does that make on a seeker? He comes to a place thinking, *I know you're going to try to make me walk an aisle, make me listen to stuff I'm not interested in, and tell me about damnation.* But then we speak his language and talk about matters of the heart that really resonate with him. In our case we did it in a loving, identifying kind of way. It was creative and it touched his life. Near the end we said, through a crisp twenty-minute message on one unified subject, "Christ is willing to help you. He'll forgive you, He'll adopt you, He'll put

His Holy Spirit in your life. It can be a whole new day."

Over three years, that original group of twenty-five blossomed into more than a thousand. We'd never seen anything like this before. We felt led by the Spirit, and we were being used in ways we never thought possible. We were young, we were foolish, we were in the middle of a modern miracle. I still look back on those years as a dream.

The core group had its own meeting, not for seekers, on Monday nights, and we prayed hard for a month about a message I was going to give seekers on a Thursday night. It was to be a simple gospel message. We prayed that all the seekers we had been adding would become Christians.

How naive we were! We thought we could just pray and preach the gospel, and that would be enough to see kids come into a relationship with Christ.

We prayed, "God, do a miracle. Bring people to Yourself. Crash through by Your Holy Spirit."

As I prepared the message, I tried to make it convincing and compelling. The Spirit kept saying to me, "Tell the story of the crucifixion and why Christ did it."

I thought, *That's not going to be flashy enough for high school students. They're going to come to hear me talk about the crucifixion?* I battled with the Lord.

Finally I said, "Okay, we'll do it Your way."

When the big night arrived, I spoke for twenty minutes, simply telling the story of the crucifixion and why it happened. At the end I said that a lot of us had been praying a long time for "you seekers who have been around here for a while, that maybe it's time some of you admitted your sin and received Christ as your Savior." I'd never given an altar call before. I wondered what to ask them to do. Stand up? They would never do that! They're with their friends; peer pressure is unbelievable.

I said, "If you'd like to receive Christ, stand up."

Immediately almost three hundred students stood. Thinking they had misunderstood, I panicked. Maybe I had asked the Christians to stand! I said, "I hope you're standing because you're acknowledging you're a sinner, and that Christ is the only way you can have your sins forgiven." Not only did they remain standing, but a few more also stood.

We were there till almost midnight, people lined up six deep waiting to pray to receive Christ.

When it was all over, I went out to the back of the church and sat on the sidewalk alone, leaning back against a red brick wall. I shook my head. *This is absolutely unbelievable. Where would all those seekers be if we hadn't designed a service for them?*

"God, thank You from the bottom of my heart for this idea of having a service for seekers. And if

You give me grace, I will do everything in my power for the rest of my life to organize a place in which seekers can search."

That night I was struck by the explosive power of the preached gospel. Seekers need to be challenged regularly, creatively, lovingly, but without apology, with the story of the crucified Christ. The cross became even more precious to me because I had seen its dynamic power when it was preached to seekers.

That night on the sidewalk I was also overwhelmed that I could be used. That God uses *me* should be the eighth wonder of the spiritual world. I still can't get over it. I feel inadequate, inarticulate, dispensable, and fragile. Apart from an infilling of the Holy Spirit, I don't have one thing to say, and no power with which to say it. And I've learned the hard way that I am so inarticulate and incapable in and of my own strength that I know better than to try to minister without God.

When He called me to start a church, I prayed, "Lord, would it be all right if we had a service for seekers, like we did with the kids?" This struck a chord so deep in me that if I hadn't felt the freedom to do that, I'd have felt my hands were bound.

I felt God was saying, "Bill, it's part of who I made you; it's how I'm pleased to use you. Have a service for seekers."

I asked God if we could also focus on a service

for believers where we would be free in the Spirit to worship and exalt and edify, to teach, to pray, to celebrate the sacraments. When I felt a green light on that idea too, it was all I needed. A decade and a half later, more than twelve thousand people attend the seekers services at Willow Creek Community Church every weekend, and thousands of believers worship on Wednesday nights.

You'll get a little better glimpse of our church later in the book, but mainly I want to concentrate on seven wonders of God's world. For this book is like our church. It is aimed at both the seeker and the convinced. If you are already convinced, may God's wonders thrill you to the point of worship. And if you are a seeker, may this rehearsal of God's greatness lead you to the end of your search.

1

You Matter to God

You have never looked into the eyes of a human being who does not matter to God. No, not even when looking in the mirror. When that truth grips you at the core of your being, you will never be the same. You will live in awe of the scope and depth and breadth of God's love, and you will treat people differently.

THE GREEKS OF THE second century B.C. compiled this list of impressive man-made structures that came to be known as the Seven Wonders of the World:

>   The Pyramids of Egypt
>   The Hanging Gardens of Babylon
>   The Temple of the Goddess Artemis
>   The Lighthouse at Alexandria
>   The Statue of Zeus
>   The Mausoleum at Halicarnassus
>   The Colossus of Rhodes—a statue of the
>   Greek sun god

Throughout history men have made other such lists, including the Seven Wonders of the Middle Ages, the Seven Natural Wonders of the World, and the Seven Modern Wonders of the World.

Well, it's time that our God received a little credit for the greatest wonders of His spiritual world.

I'd like to tell you that I consulted with pastors and Christian leaders and believers all over the world, that I sent out a questionnaire, fed all the reactions into a computer, and then did a detailed statistical analysis. The truth is that I made my own list. I trust that you will not only agree with it, but that you will also be brought closer to God through studying His wonders.

Why? Because you matter to God.

In our heart of hearts, few of us believe we are important enough to really matter to God. We know who we are. We know what we are. In our minds, only "great," "good" people like Billy Graham or Mother Teresa matter to God.

But what about a terrorist assassin? What about an international drug dealer? A Panamanian strongman? A murderous Middle Eastern "holy" man? A Chicago-based mass murderer?

Does God have much use for people like that? Don't most of us carry around a little unwritten, maybe subconscious, list of people for whom we believe God has no use? How about the guy who peddles dope to elementary school children? Child pornographers? Bribe-taking attorneys? Crooked politicians? Greedy stockbrokers?

The people we feel don't matter to God may not even be overtly evil. They may simply have a different color of skin or ethnic background. What we're saying is, in effect, "God couldn't have any use for someone like that, and neither do I."

We're All Wrong

The fact is, we're all wrong. Jesus spent a lot of time with people just like that: irreligious people, undesirables, the unconvinced, the spiritually confused, the morally bankrupt. These were the very people for whom we might assume God had no use. The Pharisees—the most conservative religious leaders of His day—thought that very thing. They huddled to the side, shook their heads, and talked among themselves. "He claims to be the Son of the Holy God, yet He associates with 'that kind' of person!"

Jesus knew exactly what they were thinking. So, He moved the whole procession nearer to the Pharisees and told three stories. It is the only time in Scripture that He told three stories in succession, and they are most interesting because they have so much in common.

First He told of the Shepherd who lost one of his one hundred sheep, left the ninety-nine, searched for and found the lost one, and brought it back to the fold. He was so happy that he called some shepherd friends around him and threw a party. What was lost had been found.

Then Jesus told the story of a woman who lost

one of her ten coins. She turned over all the furniture, lit a lamp, swept her house, and searched and searched until she found her coin. She was so glad that she called her lady friends and threw a party. What was lost had been found.

Jesus then told the story of a man who had two sons. The younger grew cocky, thought he could make it on his own, and asked his father for his inheritance ahead of time. He took it and left for a distant land where he tasted the fast lane until his money ran out. Disoriented, disenfranchised, and bankrupt, he came to his senses and headed home. He decided to apologize to his father and offer himself as a hired hand because he felt he had forfeited his right to be called a son.

While he was still a long way from his father's estate, his father saw him coming. He ran to meet his son, to embrace him and kiss him. The son tried to tell his father that he no longer felt worthy to be called a son, but the father wouldn't hear of it. Rather, he threw a party, invited his friends, killed the fatted calf, and brought out a ring and new clothes for his son. What was lost had been found.

Jesus must have been so incensed by the Pharisees' concern over who mattered to God that He decided to clear up the evil confusion once and for all. Rather than following His usual custom of telling just one story to make His point, He clarified that whether people lost one of a hundred, one of ten, or one of two items of great value, it mattered deeply to them.

The sheep mattered enough to the shepherd that he went himself to find it. He didn't say, "What's one sheep, one percent?" He searched until he found it.

The coin mattered to the woman. All her time and energy went into finding it. Perhaps she was a widow and it represented ten percent of all she had to her name.

A Missing Son Matters

It goes without saying that a missing son matters to a dad. Some years ago I received a call from a man whose twenty-four-year-old son had gone on a hunting trip and didn't return. I will never forget that father's voice when he said, "My son is missing."

Had Jesus' listeners really heard Him, they would have been crushed by the weight of His love. He was saying that seemingly insignificant things matter so much that people drop everything and search for them. They leave the others to find the one. They turn their houses upside down. They stand at the end of the lane waiting for the return of the prodigal. And when they find what they had lost, they are so happy that they throw parties.

God's love looks beyond the sins of the wandering man or woman and treasures that person. His love is so pure that it endures years of resistance, years of pleasure-seeking, money-chasing, and power-grabbing. God is saying to you, to me, to anyone who may appear undesirable, "Even though you are off the track, you matter to Me."

But, you say, even a criminal? A murderer? What did Jesus say to the repentant thief on the cross? Jesus told that thief that he would be with Him that very day in paradise. Why? Because that man mattered.

It's difficult for us to comprehend love like that, because it's so unlike your love and mine. We're finite. Our love is conditional. It has limitations.

Several years ago, when I first studied this truth that *everyone* matters to God, I tried to come to grips with what it meant in my life. I worked out at a fitness center that employed a recent Indian immigrant, a little bald guy who spoke broken English and exhibited various idiosyncrasies. Most of the clientele of that center treated him as if they had little use for him. I came to the conclusion that if everyone mattered to God, so did this man, and thus he had to matter to me.

Rather awkwardly at first, I attempted to befriend him by talking with him and trying to build an informal relationship. I kidded around with him, gave him a Christmas gift, and eventually gave him a Bible. A devout Muslim, he gave me a copy of the Koran the next day. We began to talk more and more.

When I came back from a speaking trip, I was changing clothes by my locker when he approached me. "Mr. Bill," he said, "while you were gone, my wife left me and our little child, and we are all alone. I don't know what I am going to do."

I was the only person he had told, and the pain was etched on his face. I felt a leading from the Holy Spirit to embrace him. Just as quickly I called an internal time out. I had two basic problems with the leading, and I thought the Lord should know about them. First, I'm not a naturally affectionate person, particularly with men (especially standing there in my underwear!).

Secondly, this man was not just an unbeliever; he was also actively worshiping the competition.

Still I felt a definite leading from the Lord that He wanted this man to know in the middle of his pain that he mattered to God. It was as if the Lord were saying, "I'm looking for one of My children to communicate that to him. Will you do it for Me?"

It was a big step for me, but I put my arms around the man and drew him to me. He flooded my shoulder with tears. It was a very important moment. (Devastated, he soon returned to India, to be close to friends and relatives.) When I realized how much this man mattered to God, it made him matter more to me.

A Modern Day Pharisee

I am chagrined by the number of times that I —a Christian, a minister—have done the same ugly, unthinkable thing the Pharisees did: I had a little unpublished list of people that I didn't think mattered too much: the gas station attendant, the waitress, the bellhop, the cashier, the driver, the neighbor with the barking dog, the obnoxious drunk next to me on an airplane flight, the guy who doesn't share my world view.

Those people don't really matter much, do they?

Yes, they do. They matter to God—regardless of race, salary, sex, education, religious label or lack thereof, regardless of history. Therefore, they must matter to you and me. Realizing that will have a dramatic, revolutionary effect on how we treat others, and I hope, how we see ourselves too.

You have never looked into the eyes of a human being who does not matter to God. No, not even when looking in the mirror. When that truth grips you at the core of your being, you will never be the same. You will live in awe of the scope and depth and breadth of God's love, and you will treat people differently.

Maybe you are a seeker. The fact that you're

reading this book may indicate that you are being lovingly sought out by a God—to whom you matter! He doesn't have a designer straightjacket in mind for you. He is seeking you out because He knows you need forgiveness from your sin. He knows you need liberation from guilt. He knows you need a purpose, a guide, a friend, strength for the storms of life. He says, "I'll be that to you. I'll be all of that."

You can resist God. You can make sure you don't get found. But it is not in your best interest to keep hiding. My humble counsel to you is to keep seeking and to allow God to find you. Luke 15:10 says that there is joy among the angels when one sinner comes to Christ. Whenever I read that I remember myself as a cocky, rebellious, self-willed seventeen-year-old who thought he was going to impress God with his religiosity.

But I learned that I could never string together enough righteousness to impress a holy God. I remember exactly where I was when I broke down and repented, confessed my sin, and trusted Jesus Christ to be my Savior, forgiver, and friend. The moment I did that, all of heaven erupted in a magnificent celebration. There was a party and a banner, and the name on the banner was mine.

Maybe you don't matter much to your parents. Maybe you don't matter too much to your spouse. Maybe you don't matter too much to your friends. But you matter to God more than you can imagine. He loves you. He can be trusted. He'll forgive you. He'll transform you. He'll guide you. He'll use you. And He'll satisfy you.

Stay with me and see how, as we study God's seven greatest wonders of the spiritual world.

2

God Loves Me

Sinners matter to a holy God. What a wonder! Millions throughout history have realized that though they have failed in many ways, God loves them still. They have fallen on their knees in worship and wonder as the reality of God's unconditional, forgiving love gripped their lives and stirred their souls.

WE BROUGHT HOME MY SON Todd's first two-wheeled bike on a rainy day, and I watched from the dryness of the garage as he tried it out. His saucer-like eyes and unbridled grin made a father's unique emotions wash over me. It was a profound, mountaintop experience as I stood there thinking, *There is nothing I would rather do, no place I would rather be, no greater joy I can imagine than to be able to endow my boy with this gift.* I had never gotten more fulfillment from giving anything to anybody.

While he wobbled around the driveway, I wept, and Matthew 7:11 hit me: "If you then, evil [to the core, that's me], know how to give gifts to your children, how much more shall your Father in heaven give good to those who ask Him!"

God's Inclination

There were times when I didn't ask God for certain things in prayer because I thought He wouldn't be interested. I severely and regularly underestimate God's inclination to bestow good gifts upon His children. The perfect God with unlimited resources gets joy from showering His children with blessings.

That nature of God, His unconditional love, has staggered the mind throughout history. In the First Century the apostle John wrote, "See how great a love the Father has bestowed upon us, that we should be called children of God . . . " (1 John 3:1a). Indeed, how great a love can this be that people like you and me could be brought into the family of God?

People with pasts like ours.

People with problems like ours.

Shady areas.

Skeletons in closets.

How great a love is this that we could be not only loved by God, but also brought into His very family through Christ?

Sinners matter to a holy God. What a wonder! Millions throughout history have realized that though they have failed in many ways, God loves them still. They have fallen on their knees in worship and wonder as the reality of God's unconditional, forgiving love gripped their lives and stirred their souls.

You Matter!

In chapter one, I had the unspeakable privilege of announcing that whoever you are and whatever the status of your life, you matter to God infinitely more than you think you do. If you already know that, your heart has been warmed by the reminder. But you might also just as easily be one who has heard those words—God loves people, God loves you, you matter to God—but have never experienced what they really mean.

Just as a person who hangs around the airport and watches planes doesn't necessarily know what it is to fly, you can attend church your whole life, hang around spiritual institutions, and look at people who have known and experienced the love of God without ever being deeply touched by it. If that's you, you're missing something.

I know some who once felt loved by God, but they don't sense that any more. It's a fond but fading memory. I pray that God through His Spirit will allow you to feel His love by the time you finish this chapter.

Living in the Love of the Lord

The atmosphere of your existence will change when you live in the awareness of the love of God. As you live in that love over time, your fears will subside—those free floating fears that you're going to be subjected to something that will destroy your potential for happiness.

When you live in the love of the Lord, your self-esteem grows. Why? Because if you matter to God, *you matter.* You sense a dignity about yourself, a security. In the love of the Lord you grow to where you become so secure that you can take risks you never used to take. You realize that you are loved by God enough even to experience failure and not be wiped out. You can try things you never dared before because you have the undergirding of knowing that no failure is final when you are loved by God.

When you live in the love of the Lord, you feel at peace in an uncertain world. You're optimistic about the future because you know Who holds the future. You feel understood.

I used to be hard on my wife, my friends, my staff, even the elders of the church where I pastor. They didn't seem to understand the pressures on my life. I did my best to get them to understand, but when they couldn't, or—from my vantage point—wouldn't, I harbored bitterness against them in my spirit.

But now that I've lived many years in the love of the Lord, I don't put those kinds of expectations on people. God understands me. I matter to Him. He loves me, and He understands. And that's enough.

When you live in the love of the Lord, you feel watched over, you feel protected, you feel safe, you feel approved. You sense God's smile. There's nothing like living in the love of the Lord!

A whole generation, because it has not experienced the love of the Lord, is looking for love in all the wrong places. The people of my generation look for love in singles bars, bank vaults, fun fixes, materialism, you name it. They're not finding love, so they substitute rushes, kicks, highs.

People who discover the love of the Lord and open their lives to Him see their need for love satisfied. God's perfect love meets their need so completely that instead of looking for love in all the wrong places, they spill over with love to people they didn't even care about before.

People who live in the love of the Lord have wonderful moments no one else can appreciate. One morning recently I arrived at the church at about six o'clock. I spun in my office chair and put my feet up on the credenza. I had my journal and prayer notebook, which I use every morning while praying for the congregation, my family, and others.

Just as I started to write I saw the sun's huge ball of fire rise on the eastern horizon, and my thoughts raced to Lamentations 3:22, 23: "The Lord's lovingkindnesses indeed never cease, For His compassions never fail. They are new every morning; great is Thy faithfulness."

It was as if God were saying, "Look at the sun, Bill. It's a symbol that I'm going to love you all day today, just like I did yesterday. I'm not going to run out of love. My love renews itself and commits itself to you in a fresh way every morning. You won't have to look for love today; you've got it."

That changed my outlook on the day. I like to be liked, but when I experience so clearly the love of the Lord, I don't need man's approval so much.

I could write a book on what it is like for me to live in the love of the Lord, but that's not the purpose of this book. I want you to know, really know, that God is committed to you.

How Do You Know God Loves You?

First, He says He does.
Second, He proves He does.
The first great evidence of God's love for you is that He comes right out and says it. It is no small thing to say to another human being, "I love you." That's not the thing a thinking person does carelessly. If you blurt out, "I love you," on a second

date, your love may be spurned. So, we don't do that. We start by throwing out some feelers. We say, "I like you," and we wait for a response. Then we progress to "I like you a lot." And if the person says, "I like you a lot too," we know we're headed down the right track. So we go further and say, "I love spending time with you." When the person says, "I love spending time with you too," we're almost ready. We wait for an opportunity and hold our breath, then blurt, "I love you."

That's a nervous moment. Will our love be spurned?

Along with saying, "I love you" also goes the responsibility of behaving in a way that proves it. If you say, "I love you" to someone, you'd better be prepared to back it up with action. "I love you" is a high risk pronouncement.

God's love can be spurned too. He knows what love costs and what it takes to back it up. Carefully consider that He not only says, "I love you," but that He also puts it in print. He goes on record in a Book, *the* Book. He wants you to read it and re-read it in case your heart wavers on this point.

"Do not fear, for I have redeemed you; I have called you by name; you are Mine!" (Isaiah 43:1).

"But God demonstrates His own love toward us, in that while we were yet sinners, Christ died for us" (Romans 5:8).

"I have loved you with an everlasting love;

therefore I have drawn you with lovingkindness"
(Jeremiah 31:3).

That last verse is in the Bible because some of
us might think God's love is like human love, which
runs out after a time. Disappoint somebody enough
and you get the feeling that the person is going to
run out of love. God says, in essence, "Don't ever
compare Me and My love with human love, because
Mine never runs out, though you violate it over and
over again. There's more love where that came
from." I can't count the times I've talked with people who have committed some sin and are convinced
they have provided the straw that broke the back of
God's love. That's when I have the privilege of reading to them from Jeremiah of God's everlasting love.

God the Illustrator

Over and over in His Book God says, "I love
you. You matter to me." In case people miss the
point—which we're capable of doing—God elabo-
rates by vividly illustrating His love.

Elizabeth Barrett Browning wrote: "How do I
love thee? Let me count the ways. I love thee to the
depth and breadth and height my soul can reach
. . . and if God should choose I shall but love thee
better after death." The poet is saying, "Let me illustrate, let me make you understand how much I
love you."

God goes to amazing lengths to illustrate, to underscore the breadth of His love for us. He seems to provide an illustration for people in every walk of life. For the astronomer, the space buff, the scientist, he says, "For as high as the heavens are above the earth, so great is His lovingkindness toward those who fear him" (Psalm 103:11).

God uses another illustration for animal lovers. Jesus compared His love to the concern that a hen has for her chicks (Matthew 23:37 and Luke 13:34). In the Old Testament references are made to the ferocious loyalty a mother bear feels for her cubs: "I will encounter them like a bear robbed of her cubs, and I will tear open their chests; There I will also devour them like a lioness, as a wild beast will tear them" (Hosea 13:8). "Let a man meet a bear robbed of her cubs, rather than a fool in his folly" (Proverbs 17:12).

Maybe you're neither a space buff nor an animal lover. Perhaps you're a mother. God likens His love to the kind of love a nursing mother has for the child at her breast: "Can a woman forget her nursing child, and have no compassion on the son of her womb? Even these may forget, but I will not forget you" (Isaiah 49:15). Though that doesn't apply to me, it sure gets my wife's attention. I'll always remember seeing the look in Lynne's eyes while she was cradling, loving, talking to, and praying over our kids as she nursed them.

To reach me, God likens His love to the love of a father for his son or daughter: "Just as a father has compassion on his children, so the Lord has compassion on those who fear Him" (Psalm 103:13).

Maybe you're not a space buff, an animal lover, or even a child lover. God asks if you have a friend, or if you understand what friendship is. He says, "Greater love has no one than this, that one lay down his life for his friends" (John 15:13).

The Lord says, "I love you, and I'll be a better friend to you than any friend you have. I laid down My life for you."

The Lord not only comes out and says, "I love you," but He also illustrates it in creative ways so anyone can glimpse into God's heart and have his being exploded with that love.

The Proof

You might say, "Talk is cheap. So what if He says it? Does He show it?" God has been showing His love to people from the beginning.

He showed His love to Adam and Eve by giving them a second chance after the fall.

He showed His love to Noah and his family by sparing them from the flood.

He showed His love to Abraham by producing a ram for the sacrifice, instead of making him sacrifice Isaac, his son.

He showed His love to David by forgiving his sin with Bathsheba.

He showed His love for Job by ending Satan's attack and giving Job twice as much as he had before he endured his testing.

He showed His love to the disciples through the teaching/companionship ministry of Jesus, His Son.

Through His healing and loving touch, Jesus showed His love to lepers and the blind, the lame, the deaf, and the hungry.

God showed His love for the world once and for all in the most dramatic way possible, by offering His most precious Son as a sin sacrifice for nondeserving people like you and me. The blood-stained cross stands today as the ultimate symbol of the act of love.

Your Part

God doesn't just shower His love on the world. He also showers His love on you. Since you were born, God has reached out to you. He has protected you and has limited Satan's attacks in ways you'll never know. He has offered you communication, guidance, and His salvation. He offers you a home in heaven.

God not only says, "I love you," but He also demonstrated it in history, and He continues to demonstrate it by the way He extends Himself to us all our lives. The issue that remains is how you respond to God's great love. The Scripture says people respond in one of two ways. They either treasure His love or they trample it.

When some people discover that God loves them with a perfect love, they open their lives to it. They say, "I accept it, I receive it, I am melted by it, I am moved by it. Lord, thank You! Thank You!" They heave a sigh of relief, they relax in God's love, and then, without being coerced or manipulated, they burst forth in spontaneous worship and return God's love. They want to serve and please and honor the Lord.

That, friend—the discovery of the love of God, the acceptance of it, and then the return of that love—is the miraculous exchange out of which flows the dynamic energy, strength, and power of the Christian life. In the church where that dynamic is evident, there is no need to manipulate or coerce people to serve.

People offend me when they compliment me on "getting people" involved in the ministries of our church. I wasn't in ministry one day before I decided that I would not "get" people to do things through manipulation. If that was the ministry, I wanted out. I don't manipulate. That's not our church's game plan. I try to convince people that they are loved by God with a perfect love. I try to convince sinners that they matter to God.

When sinners discover they matter to God, when they find out they're loved with an everlasting love, when they realize their failures can be forgiven and their sins cleansed, they *want* to return that love. All we do is suggest biblical ways for the love to be expressed.

If God's love is overflowing in your heart, spill some on your spouse. Spill some on your kids. Spill some on your parents. Spill some on the people at work. If you find yourself wanting to serve God with your time and your talents and your treasures, do it! That's a natural, loving response to His love for you.

Remember, our work for Him should be done only out of gratitude for the love He has shown us. We cannot buy salvation or even come close to paying Him back. "We love, because He first loved us" (1 John 4:19).

I've been in ministry a long time, and I'm more motivated now than ever. Why? Because I know more of the love of the Lord now, and the more I understand the extent of its height, depth, and breadth, the more I want to worship Him and serve Him and relax in His love. I want His love to spill out to other people.

Treasure or Trample?

You may ask how people wind up in hell if God is a loving God. People wind up in hell by trampling the love of God instead of treasuring it. They ignore it, spurn it, yawn over it, close their hearts to it, keep saying "someday, someday, someday."

The Bible says there will be a someday. It's a day of reckoning. To those who have spurned His love, God will say in effect, "I loved you every day of your life. I loved you with a perfect love. I extended Myself to you. I made My wisdom available to you. I made My comfort and My strength and My Spirit available to you. I made My offer of salvation to you. But you trampled and spurned My love. You had it your way on earth, so now you can have it your way in eternity."

Are you facing that scenario? Will you continue to trample the love of God? That's the question of the ages, and it is one you yourself must answer. Open your heart to the love of the Lord and say, "I need it, God. Touch me." He will touch you and enable you to repent of your sin and place your personal faith in Jesus Christ. He forgives you and becomes the mediator who makes you acceptable before God.

How I pray that you would not just know, but would also feel and live in and relax in and enjoy the love of the Lord—the perfect, unconditional, unlimited love of God.

That decision, that step, seems risky. But as we will see, God can be trusted.

3

God Can Be Trusted

Have you proven God trustworthy? Have you gone out on a limb, taken faith steps, and trusted Him in your daily life, or are you sitting on your hands theorizing about God's trustworthiness? Has His trustworthiness failed for you, or has it simply been untried? Don't tell me God hasn't been trustworthy if you haven't tried Him. Test God and you will find His Word is true: He can be trusted.

As I WALKED TOWARD the plane for my first sky diving attempt, I patted the parachute of the fellow in front of me and asked, "Do you think these will open the way they say they will?"

He turned and shot back, "In about five minutes, we're both going to find out, aren't we?"

What a simple truth: the only way to find out if a parachute is going to work is to jump out of a plane and pull the ripcord. We didn't prove those parachutes on the ground. We had to jump.

The second of the greatest wonders of the spiritual world is that our God can be trusted. But unless you are willing to jump—unless you are willing to test God, His trustworthiness will be simply a useless, unproven, theological theory, rather than a powerful, personal, life-changing reality.

There are few subjects I feel more strongly

about than God's trustworthiness. I have banked my life on it. Shortly after I became a Christian in my late teens, I was challenged to memorize Proverbs 3:5–6: "Trust in the Lord with all your heart, and do not lean on your own understanding. In all your ways acknowledge Him, and He will make your paths straight."

The promise at the end of that passage is that He will direct your life, He will "make your paths straight." *Prove* Him to be trustworthy. *Follow* Him. *Listen* to His leadings. Jump from the plane. See whether He is trustworthy.

God loves me. He promises that if I will yield my life to Him and open myself to His leadership, He will direct me consistent with His highest hopes for me. He knows me better than anybody knows me. He knows what will fulfill me, challenge me, motivate me, make me flourish.

I was young and somewhat naive spiritually when I accepted the challenge to memorize those verses. I decided to make a faith covenant with God (you might call it a faith gamble). I remember saying to myself in the presence of the Lord, "I am going to trust the Lord with all my heart. I am not going to rely on my own instincts. I am just going to try to please the Lord in every way that I can, and I will see if He directs my life. I'll take a shot. I'll jump. I'll see what happens."

But . . .

In making this covenant with the Lord, I put a little tag on the end, saying, "Lord, I will trust You until You prove Yourself untrustworthy. Then I'm done. All bets are off. I will reassume responsibility for my own life and future. I will make my own paths straight. But I will first play this whole thing out as long as I can. I am going to trust You with all my heart and see if You will lead my life." I had no idea the ride God had planned for me. I didn't know that He enjoys and excels at scripting adventure plots and plugging people like you and me into them.

The last fifteen or so years of my life make a parachute jump look like a walk in the park. It's been amazing. When I made my faith gamble, my life was neatly arranged. I didn't expect God to change what I had planned. I would finish college with an economics and business administration major. I would assume ownership of the family produce business. I would find a nice Dutch girl with blond hair and blue eyes and marry her. We would have three or four blue-eyed, blond-haired Dutch kids. I would atend a little Christian Reformed church, give some money now and then, and buy lots of toys for myself (and a few for the kids). I would lead the all-American life, pursue the all-American dream. I had everything planned, until I trusted the Lord with all my heart.

It was as if God said, "All right, let's see if you

mean business. Let's see if you will really trust Me."

The first adventure came when He led me, very strongly and unmistakably in my spirit, to consider leaving the family business, leaving my hometown and family, and heading out to a different place. God doesn't call many people *out* of the marketplace into Christian work. He calls most people to be an influence for Christ *in* the marketplace. But in my case, He had something else in mind. I didn't know this at the time; I could just feel that He was leading me out of the well-established business I was expected to take over some day.

I loved the marketplace. From what others told me, I was good at it. I had a good future, a lot of responsibility at a young age. But as I prayed and trusted God, it became clear that He wanted me out. I went to my Dad's corner office one day—he was a Christian and president of the company—and said, "Dad, I have made a faith commitment to the Lord that I will trust Him with my whole life and depend on Him to lead and direct me. He is directing me out of this business into something else."

My dad said, "Is that right? That's a good thing, then. You need to do that. But let me remind you of a few things: If you walk out, there may not be doors open for you if you ever decide to come back. Ownership of the company will probably not be in the cards again for you in the future. And those company credit cards in your wallet, the cars and airplanes you have access to, all that stays here. But if God is leading you a different way, go ahead. As long as we're clear."

Dad wasn't saying, "Back off and quit being a Christian." He was a smart man. I believe he simply wanted to jar me a little and make sure I had counted the entire cost. He had worked thirty-five years to build a business he was proud to be able to hand over to his son. Did I really want to give that up?

A Divine Demotion

Sobered, I did what any nineteen-year-old spiritual giant would do. I said, "Well, Dad, I may have jumped the gun on this. It's possible that I got my wires crossed and got a little overly enthusiastic. Let me go back and pray a little more about this."

I walked out of his office thinking, *This is very serious.* I wanted to trust the Lord with all my heart, but was I ready for what looked to me like a divine demotion? The more I thought and prayed about it, the more I knew it would be unthinkable to cop out at the first test.

I went back to my Dad and told him, "I am going to do it. I'm going to leave." I walked out of his office for the last time, leaving the keys, the credit cards, the toys, and the possibility of ownership. I felt very sober, but I also had a sense that God was up to something. I didn't know what.

I had been offered an entry-level position in a Christian youth organization, so I moved from Kalamazoo to Chicago. I became a shipping clerk earning minimum wage. Standing at a conveyor belt between two middle-aged women, I put products in little boxes, eight hours a day, five days a week for a year.

I had no real responsibility. It was tedious, repetitive production work. I didn't know what God was up to, but I knew I needed to continue to trust Him. There is a strange sense of fulfillment when you trust God. Everything else might feel unsettled, but if you know you're in tune with God, it's all right.

At the end of that year, the leadership of the church I attended in Park Ridge, Illinois, told me thay had a position open for someone to work with high school students. "It is a full-time position," they told me, "but we can only offer half-time pay." There was a pattern developing. From generous expense accounts to minimum wage to half-time pay for full-time work, this was another divine demotion. But I believed God was in it, so I started working at that church.

Talk about an adventure! Starting with twenty-five or thirty kids, over the course of three years, we saw God miraculously grow a youth group to a thousand high school students. Kids' lives were changed, and when they brought their parents on Parents' Night, many of them also found Christ.

My new wife Lynne and I owned a two-bedroom house a few blocks from the church, and we intended to stay there the rest of our lives. But then God led again. I felt an unmistakable leading in my spirit that I was to start a church for non-churched people. And I was to start the church from nothing —no people, no buildings, no land, and no salary. That fit my pattern perfectly. I had become accustomed to going down the corporate ladder.

The Birth of a Church

In 1975, with a few other friends, we went door to door in the northwest suburbs of Chicago eight hours a day, six days a week for a month, asking people, "Do you actively attend a local church?"

If they said yes, we said, "Fine, thanks."

If they said no, we asked why. We tabulated their responses, and from that we shaped our programming plans.

We had no money, but we had to pay the first month's rent for our offices and for the theater where we planned to hold our Sunday services. The only business I knew was selling produce, so I bought a truckload of tomatoes from our company in Michigan. The high school kids and I went door to door selling tomatoes. We used the profit for those initial bills and ministry support. Some of us worked other jobs at night, our wives worked, and we took in boarders to help pay the rent. It was an adventure, and we knew God was in it.

The Weaning

I look back on those days and I know what I didn't know then. That series of divine demotions was necessary because God knew I wouldn't be usable unless I was weaned from two forces that had a grip on my life. I hadn't been aware of it, but I had a love for power and a love for money. Most of my previous decisions had been based on those priorities. Through the divine demotions, God stripped those things from me. When I was laid bare, when I had no power and no money, I sensed God saying, "Maybe now I can use you."

Since then, there have been hundreds of adventures—purchasing one hundred acres of land, building an auditorium and classrooms, starting new ministries, and assembling a staff. It has been wonderful. I can now say with great confidence that God can be trusted. It's not just theory. Dynamic power can be released in you if you determine to trust God with your life.

I have reached the conclusion that God can be trusted with my life. Have you reached the same conclusion for yourself? When you entrust your life to a trustworthy God, you can relax and say, "He knows best. He sees the whole picture. I can trust Him to lead me down the right path."

Have you proven God trustworthy? Have you gone out on a limb, taken faith steps, and trusted Him in your daily life—or are you sitting on your hands theorizing about God's trustworthiness? Has His trustworthiness failed for you, or has it simply been untried? Don't tell me God hasn't been trustworthy if you haven't tried Him. Test God and you will find His Word is true: He can be trusted.

Where Do I Start?

Begin by trusting God with your eternal destiny. God put within us the sense that there must be a purpose to all of this. There must be an afterlife that gives this life perspective. But ask ten people, "If there is a heaven, who goes there?"

Nine of ten will say, "Those who attempt to lead a good, moral life. Those who don't hurt others."

It only stands to reason that people think this way, but the Bible crashes through with the truth. God has said, "I am Holy. The only way to gain entrance into the kingdom of heaven is for you to be absolutely holy." His standard of behavior is perfection. Are you wondering whether you've lived an absolutely holy life? Talk to your spouse. Ask your mother or dad. Ask your kids. Check it out. The Bible will tell you. None of us have led holy lives. Granted, some live a little better than others. But nobody has come close to perfection. "There is none righteous, not even one" (Romans 3:10).

"For all have sinned and fall short of the glory of God" (Romans 3:23).

No amount of good deeds can erase our record of violations against God's holiness. Once the standard of moral perfection has been broken, nothing you do will change that fact.

Help, I Need Somebody

The Bible says you need someone who can change your record, erase your violations, cover your mistakes, make you acceptable to a holy God. Jesus Christ is that Someone. He absorbed your punishment on the cross. He erases sin and cleanses transgressions. He offers you a clean slate. Someday He will present you as holy and blameless before a holy and blameless God, at which time you will be acceptable to God and you will spend eternity with Him.

You can't change your record. You need a savior, and a Savior has been provided. At some point you must trust what somebody else did for you rather than trust what you think you can do for yourself. There must be a trust transfer for you to gain eternal life. If you were to stand before God and He were to ask, "On what basis do you expect to be granted entrance into the kingdom of heaven?", what would your answer be?

Some would say, "I know I'm a sinner, but I am trusting in the work of Another. I am trusting in what Jesus did for me. I am trusting that He has cleansed me from my sin—that He has erased my past. I am trusting that He has made me acceptable to You, God. I am trusting Christ for salvation and eternal life. On that basis, on His merits, I appeal to you for entrance into the kingdom of heaven."

Others will say, "I should be admitted to heaven because even though I slipped up a bit, I tried hard to be a good guy, and I tried to be a faithful spouse and church attender." But as you list those reasons, your heart will sink. Those reasons will seem so insufficient that your mind will reel, and you will say remorsefully, "I see it now. I should have trusted Christ. I should have banked on His provision for me. I should have taken the risk and proved Him trustworthy for salvation."

The Provision

A friend who knew I needed a rest gave me an airline ticket to a resort. He was careful to tell me, "Your room has been taken care of. Charge your meals to the room. I have also provided for you to attend a dinner show." After I had rested for a few days, the time came for me to go to that show. I stood in line down a long hall. I had been instructed to just say the name of this individual to the host, and he would let me have a seat in the crowded auditorium. In front of me were fifty or sixty well-dressed people.

I began to worry. What if I got up there and the guy didn't know the name of the individual who sent me? The people in front of me were having animated conversations with the host and leaving in a huff. As I got closer, I could hear the host. "You don't understand. We are all sold out. There is no more room." Some were offering him one-hundred-dollar bills.

I had only twenty dollars. Obviously, I would not be buying my way in. As I got closer and closer, people were leaving very angrily. The man directly in front of me left with two one-hundred-dollar bills in his hand. Nervously, I went up and said quietly, "Mr. _____ said he made provisions for me."

"What is your name?"

I told him, and he said, "Come with me."

That was the only way! There was no other way to get into that place. The person who made the difference had provided for me.

On the authority of God's Word I can say that there is only one way anybody will gain entrance into the kingdom of God, and that is the provision made by Jesus Christ. "Jesus said to him, 'I am the way, and the truth, and the life; no one comes to the Father, but through Me'" (John 14:6). Every single person who would go to heaven must make a transfer of trust from what he plans on doing for himself to what Christ did for him.

Have you come to the point where you have said, "I cannot ever earn my way; I must rely on Jesus"? He has done something for you that you cannot do for yourself. It takes a lot of humility for a self-made American to receive eternal life as a gift, but it is the only way.

When you trust Christ for your eternal destiny, He will prove Himself to be trustworthy. Nobody has ever turned to Christ for salvation and been denied. Try it. Take off your coat of cynicism and trust Christ. Prove Him to be trustworthy. Not only will He save, but He will also transform you. He will make all things new over time. I say it again, He can be trusted.

There's More

After you trust Christ for your eternal destiny, you'll discover that His trustworthiness doesn't stop there. He can also be trusted to help you:

Build a marriage.
Improve relationships.
Handle money.

Resolve conflict.
Overcome anxiety.
Deal with anger.
Find wisdom!

When people say the Bible is irrelevant, I say they haven't read it. It is the most relevant Book ever written! Every issue that touches life's deepest core is discussed in the Bible. Wisdom from God is available.

It all comes down to this: Do you trust the wisdom revealed in the Book? Do you put it into action? It may sound illogical. It may sound outdated. It may sound old-fashioned. But take a faith gamble. Jump! Trust the wisdom of God and see what happens. He will prove trustworthy every time. You can build your life on the wisdom of God's Word.

Right now you may be thinking about who you're going to marry or what vocation you'll pursue. Maybe you are thinking about a job change. A church change. Adding to your family. Making investments. Tough business issues.

Our lives are so complex these days. But God says, "I can help you. Trust Me and I will prove Myself. I will direct your life in ways that will fulfill you and challenge you and motivate you and inspire you and satisfy you." It's not theory. It's reality. But it must be tried.

Take a moment now and say, "Lord, I want to learn to trust You more than I ever have before. I want to trust You with my life." Maybe you need to make that trust transfer with respect to your eternal destiny. Maybe you are like nine of ten people who say, "I'll get to heaven by being good and trying to please God." It's a dead-end road, friend. You can't do enough. You can never be holy enough. You have to be forgiven and made holy, and that can only be done through Christ. Pray, "I know that I am a sinner. I need a Savior, and now I am choosing to trust the work of another person for my hope for salvation, my hope for eternal life. Christ is the only way and I am going to trust Him."

Trust in the Lord with all your heart. He will exceed your expectations.

4

God Forgives Me

The third of the greatest wonders of the spiritual world is that God wants to forgive you of your failure — no matter what it is. He wants to liberate you from the grasp of guilt and remorse. Are you interested? God would like to liberate you. You can be free!

SYMBOLS OF SUCCESS are displayed somewhere in almost every home. In the hall may be plaques or awards of excellence. In the den you might see a college or graduate school diploma. In the family room you might see a football trophy or track ribbons from days gone by. You might see pictures of your host or hostess with important people.

Seldom found in someone's home is anything which reminds that person of failure. Symbols of failure are usually tucked away in a closet, an attic, or a trunk in the basement. In one of those well hidden enclaves you might find a wedding ring—the painful symbol of a failed marriage. Or in the back of a file cabinet you might find some stationery or calling cards for a business that went sour. We do our best, don't we, to keep our symbols of failure out of sight and out of mind? Perhaps that is as it should be.

One of my most significant symbols of failure, however, is on display every week. It represents an embarrassing, painful failure and at the same time it represents for me a symbol of hope. Until I told them about it a couple of years ago, not even my congregation—or my wife!—knew what it was, though they saw it every week as they came into our church. Every time I see this symbol it gives me a shot of pain and regret. But immediately thereafter, by God's grace, the same symbol signals hope and power. It's a reminder of God's forgiveness.

Believe it or not, it's my pulpit. About three-and-a-half or four feet high, maybe two-and-a-half feet wide, it's made of see-through acrylic. For years I never told anybody where it came from, and no one ever asked. The Saturday night before I told the congregation, Lynne and I were flying back from Mexico. She asked me what I was planning to speak about the next morning. I said, "My pulpit."

She said, "You have Montezuma's revenge, don't you?"

Keeping My Balance

The story of my plexiglass pulpit and why it is both a symbol of failure and a harbinger of hope begins with the origins of the church where I pastor. The church started in a movie theater in 1975, and I spoke every Sunday without a pulpit, without notes, without much preparation, and frankly without much balance. A nucleus of ten or fifteen families had given up everything to start the church. We were way out on the limb of faith and we were working seven-day, eighty-hour weeks, trying to get the church organized and functioning to serve people meaningfully.

I was left with little time to study and prepare sermons. I felt extremely responsible for my own family's well-being, as well as the well-being of the other core families. Beyond that, I wondered constantly whether the church was viable. Would people who had given up on God and the church years ago really come? Would they discover God's love, His grace, and His saving and transforming power? Would people mean business in their relationships with God and be energized by Him to handle the challenges of life? Was it going to work, or was the venture futile?

So with the work and the worry, I not only gave hastily prepared sermons (superficial at best), but also unbalanced sermons. What I was preaching was true, but it was not the whole truth. Imbalanced teaching and preaching can ruin a church and, more importantly, lives—it can confuse and scar people deeply. In the early years of Willow Creek Community Church, I was guilty of imbalanced teaching. I made continual references to God's unconditional acceptance of who we are, regardless of what we do, what we say, how we live. I would say, "You can't make God love you less, no matter how often you sin, even if you repeat the sin over and over again. Even when it's a premeditated sin, if you confess it, God will smile and forgive and take you back. Where sin abounds, grace abounds more."

Understand, everything I said was absolutely true—it came right out of the Word of God. It was good doctrine. Unfortunately, it was presented without balance. Consequently, some people of the church just didn't care about the holiness of God. How could they? They didn't hear about the righteousness of God. They didn't hear about the seriousness of sin and the scars it leaves. Nor did they hear much about justice. They just heard a lot about acceptance and grace.

I didn't realize the problem until some people in leadership and some throughout the church became involved in serious sin. When I tried to confront them privately, their sincere response often went like this:

"God will forgive me."

"I'm still acceptable to Him, no matter what I do."

"His grace is greater than all my sins."

"I'm human, He knows that."

"He's a loving God—you preached that."

"I can't do anything to make Him love me less —He will take me back if I sin all the time, every day."

Sadly, Willow Creek went through a very painful era as the effects of immature, hastily prepared, imbalanced teaching took their toll. Several leaders left the church and many members of the congregation vanished with them. Misunderstandings, accusations, and suspicion abounded. I felt my life and dreams caving in, and as I sought the Lord, He made it clear that a teacher reaps what he sows. It was as though God were saying, "You made this bed, now lie in it. It's your fault. Blame it on the immaturity of others, blame it on sinful creatures, blame it on this, blame it on that. The fact is, it's your fault. You are the teacher."

That was the costly price of imbalanced teaching, and it was a devastating realization for me. I had to work through the ordeal on my own because I hadn't yet learned the importance of being close and accountable to Christian brothers. It was an intensely lonely, soul-wrenching time, and I felt a depth of guilt I never knew existed. I had gotten into my share of trouble in high school, and into more than my share in college. But the guilt I felt then was kid's stuff compared to this.

I had failed God by representing Him inaccurately before people, and I felt deep pangs of guilt. Not only did I feel foolish, I felt remorseful and embarrassed. Frequently I broke down before the Lord and said, "You're absolutely right. It's my fault. I was more concerned about people liking this church and becoming a part of it than I was about their understanding the true identity of God. I distorted who You are to make You more acceptable to them. God, I am so sorry. It's my fault. I am the man. Take me out. Put me back into the marketplace where I belong. I should have stayed there in the first place."

A surprising thing happened when I owned up and admitted my sinfulness before the Lord. In my spirit I sensed God saying, "I can forgive you. I can forgive you for failing Me. I am the gracious God you've been preaching about. I'm also the holy, righteous, just God you've been ignoring. But My holiness doesn't diminish My willingness to forgive you."

In my spirit I resisted that voice. I couldn't believe God could forgive me for that failure. Again and again the Holy Spirit impressed upon me, "Not only do I want to forgive you, but I also want to give you a second chance. I want you to teach truth, to represent Me accurately from here on out. Get up! Get up! Receive My forgiveness. Get on with your life. Here's a second chance, with My grace and power. Do it right this time."

When I could no longer resist that movement inside me, I said, "Lord, if I do accept this, and if

You do give me that second chance, I am going to prepare messages properly. I am going to pray more thoroughly than ever. I am going to study longer. I will write out sermons word for word. I will teach the truth. I will be balanced. To the best of my ability, I will never misrepresent You again."

Forgiven!

Those worship-filled commitments were motivated by the fact that I could be forgiven for such colossal failure. I didn't make those commitments to receive forgiveness. I had nothing to plead but guilt, but the Lord said, "I'll forgive, because I'm a gracious, forgiving God."

When I sensed His amazing grace and His offer of a second chance, I said, "It's going to be different, Lord. I'll show You how grateful I am for Your forgiveness."

This encounter with God was so significant that I decided to do what the saints in the Old Testament did. When God marked the life of an Old Testament leader, he immediately collected and stacked rocks as an altar, then named it. Sometimes he even put a name plate on it, and when he passed by it with his family, he stopped and sat with his children and said, "This is where God marked my life."

When Joshua led the nation of Israel across the Jordan River, God stopped the waters. The people crossed on dry land, past the priests who stood in the middle holding the Ark of the Covenant. The Lord instructed Joshua to choose one man from each of the twelve tribes to carry a stone from the middle of the Jordan—where the priests had stood —and to stack them on the other side as a memorial. The Israelites were told that when their children asked what the stones meant, they were to tell them of the miracle the Lord had performed that day (Joshua 4:1–24).

What kind of altar could I build to show God that this moment in time marked me, that I meant business, and that I was thankful for His forgiveness and the second chance? It came to me that I needed a pulpit. I had never had one before. I didn't even know where you got them. All I knew was that it would be a symbol of stability, balance, and accurate teaching of the whole counsel of God. A staff member suggested a glass one because we were building a church that had a lot of glass.

We found a shop that did custom acrylic work, so I headed there one afternoon. I wanted it done right now! On the way, I listened to a tape someone had given me just the week before. It was called, "Where Have All the Faithful Teachers Gone?" That tape tore me up. The speaker talked about ear-ticklers and those who were more interested in building a church than building the truth about God into individual lives. I was guilty on every count.

By the time I reached the acrylic shop, God had worked me over so thoroughly I was still misty and choked up. When a man strolled out of the back room and asked if he could help me, I said, "I need a pulpit!"

He said, "Settle down! You need an aspirin or anything?"

I said, "I need a pulpit! It's a long story and I don't have time to go into it, but I need one. I don't know how long it takes, and I don't care how much it costs. I'm Dutch, and when I say I don't care how much something costs, it means I'm on the brink of delirium, so you must understand how important this is to me."

I gave him the particulars and he said he would do his best. As I drove back to the office I played that tape again and kept saying, "God, I'll be a faithful teacher. I want to be one! You have forgiven me for my failure. You're giving me a second chance. I'm going to prepare for every message like it's the World Series and I'm up to bat. I don't care if it's in front of 5 people, 1,500, 2,500, or 8,000. When I am called to teach, I am going to be prepared and I am going to pray and I am going to be balanced. I am going to be accountable to the elders."

Between services every Sunday now, the elders give their analyses of my first message to one elder who summarizes their concerns on a sheet of paper, which I take to my office and study before the next service. I submit myself to the suggestions of the elders about what I said, because I don't even trust my own ability to be balanced anymore. Part of the problem early in my ministry was that I didn't take seriously the watch/care role of our elders. I learned the hard way that I need counselors to help give me affirmation or correction.

Every time I approach that pulpit, I sense the Holy Spirit saying, "You'd better be a faithful teacher, because you are forgiven. You got a second chance." That pulpit is a symbol of my failure, and it is also a symbol of a new commitment, a new beginning. Since I started using it, many have told me that my teaching has been helpful. They have told me they are getting stronger in their faith. Some have told me they have come to Christ at our church.

That pulpit is a symbol of God's grace to me, a symbol of hope, a symbol of a second chance. And I don't take it lightly. I was once invited to speak to a secular group made up of 500 company presidents and their spouses. I was told by other speakers at the conference that I was the first pastor who had ever been invited. I was to speak on adversity and conflict resolution.

My first session, which was on adversity, drew a group of thirty or forty executives, and I talked about how to stay steady in a storm. At one point, I said, "Friends, I've got to tell you my conviction on this: if you're going to stay steady in a storm, you've got to have a faith that is real. Real faith means being rightly related to God through the person of Jesus Christ."

After the session one of the other speakers—an economist from New York City—pulled me off to the side and said, "Do you want to be well-received here? Let me give you a little instruction. Go easy on the God stuff. I'm a Christian too, but when I speak here, I keep that pretty much to myself."

"I can't do that," I said.

"Well, then you probably won't be invited back."

"You know," I said, "I'd rather this organization leave me out than have me leave God out. I've gone that other route. I know that game. I can't play it anymore."

His advice only served to motivate me all the more. When it was appropriate in my last two sessions and I felt the leading from the Lord, I told those executives exactly what my beliefs and convictions were. I didn't say I expected them to take action right then. But I said, "You will stand accountable for your relationship with God someday, and so will I. You do what you have to do, but I am telling you, as for me and my house, we're going to make our relationship with God our number one priority."

God blessed. My sessions nearly doubled each time, and I had countless conversations in the hallway. The president of a company that employs 33,000 people pulled me aside and asked me how he could receive Christ. I left that conference with a clean conscience, and when I walked into the church auditorium the next Sunday, I saw my pulpit. I was so glad I had been forgiven, and I am still motivated by the grace that's been afforded to me. Having been forgiven for my failure, I am determined not to cave in anymore.

That was a lengthy illustration, but I hope this true story will focus God's telescope and microscope on your heart. Be as honest with yourself as you can be. Don't chicken out now! Don't rationalize anymore. How have you failed God? I'm not asking you *if* you have. We all have. "For all have sinned and fall short of the glory of God" (Romans 3:23).

The Torture Chamber

Have you failed Him in a relationship? Is there strife, anger, a private war going on with your parents, friends, associates, or spouse? Are you failing God in a relationship because you're stubborn and angry?

Have you failed God in a marriage? Are you failing Him now in a marriage?

Have you failed God or are you failing Him with your kids? Have you been too strict? Too lenient? Are you gone too much?

Have you failed God with your temper, with greed, dishonesty, pride, jealousy, profanity?

Have you failed God through sexual sin?

Or through not worshiping Him, or not giving to Him, or not serving Him as you should?

How have you failed God?

God is holy, righteous, and just. He does not take sin lightly. It cost Him the life of His Son Jesus. Because you are made in His image and because you live in His world, when you fail God, you know it. You feel guilty. Some feel more guilty than others, but we all feel a measure of guilt. That is a rotten way to live, isn't it? You may know well that torture chamber of guilt and remorse.

The third of the greatest wonders of the spiritual world is that God wants to forgive you of your failure—no matter what it is. He wants to liberate you from the grasp of guilt and remorse. Are you interested? God would like to liberate you. You can be free!

How?

First, God asks for a clear admission of your wrongdoing. Don't mince words. Don't blame anybody else. No matter how painful, you must step out from the shadows of self-deception and self-protection. God demands that you see the truth about yourself. Say, "I am the one. I have sinned. I have failed You, Lord."

He doesn't ask you to belabor it or crucify yourself. He just says, "Speak the truth to Me."

Say, "I had choices, and I made wrong ones. I admit it, and I own it." Can you say that, or are you going to jump back into the shadows? It's your choice.

Secondly, God says if you want forgiveness, entrust your failures, mistakes, and wrongdoings to Christ. He alone can forgive them. The human propensity is to bargain with God. We say, "Wipe my slate clean, because I am promising that it will be different in the future. I won't do it again." Do you ever do that? What you commit to in the future, friend, doesn't change your past. You can live like an altar boy for the rest of your life, but it doesn't change your checkered past.

Don't bargain with God. He doesn't accept deals. He needs no bargain. Don't bother making wild pledges and commitments to earn your own forgiveness. We cannot cleanse ourselves! What's done is done and we can't change it! Admit and own your sin and entrust it to the only One who can do anything about it.

When Jesus died on the cross and said, "It is finished," He was saying, "I paid the price for those sins. You entrust those sins to me, and I'll deal with them. I'll forget them completely. But I am the only One who can. I am the only One who will."

Some years ago, a man called me after midnight, desperate for counsel. He had committed a grave sin and pleaded with me to meet him. When I arrived he kept admitting his sinfulness and owning it, and then he made all kinds of pledges so God would forgive him. I said, "Friend, you are wasting your breath. You can't keep the commitments you're making. And no matter what you promise, that doesn't change the sin you have committed. You have to entrust that to the person of Jesus Christ, who is the only One who can and will blot it out, forgive it, and cleanse it."

He finally understood and by faith prayed and accepted God's forgiveness. The next day he called me at my office. He said, "On the way home I turned on the car radio, found a Christian station, and heard 'Amazing grace, how sweet the sound that saved a wretch like me.' I pulled over, rested my head on the dashboard, and cried. I finally understood. I can't earn forgiveness. I receive it as a gift. Because God loves me, He forgave me by His grace."

A Few Classics

Once you trust God to forgive you, then you need to get up and proceed with your life as though God indeed has forgiven you. We are tempted to say, "I don't feel forgiven," so God put in His Word some classic forgiveness promises you can memorize:

The *amnesia* promise: ". . . I will forgive their iniquity, and their sin I will remember no more" (Jeremiah 31:34). God says, "What was that sin you think I didn't forgive? I don't even remember it. It's done. It's gone."

The *stain removal* promise: "Though your sins are as scarlet, they will be as white as snow; though they are red like crimson, they will be like wool" (Isaiah 1:18).

The *East-West* promise: "As far as the east is from the west, so far has He removed our transgressions from us" (Psalm 103:12).

The *deep sea* promise: "Thou wilt cast all their sins into the depths of the sea" (Micah 7:19).

When a voice whispers, "God didn't forgive you; you still have some X's on the slate," use one of the forgiveness promise verses.

Say, "No, it's gone!" As you receive God's forgiveness, you are going to find that because of His amazing grace, because the slate is clean, because He takes the guilt away and gives you another chance, you will walk with a new humility.

People often assume that I must have a problem with pride because of the growth of our church. In all honesty, I am broken and humbled by what God has done. No one is more overwhelmed at what God is doing through me than I am, and no one knows better than I how weak and how close to the edge of my ability I am.

I'm also overwhelmed by my own depravity and God's grace in using me at all. On the best day of my life, I deserve hell. A friend of mine recently told me, "You have an amazing grasp of the depth of your own depravity." It's true. It amazes me that God can use someone with my background, sinfulness, and rough edges. I know my failures. The only reason I am being used is that I'm working for a forgiving God.

His forgiveness makes us more humble, more worshipful, more tolerant of other people's failures. And it should make us quicker to forgive. Woe to any man or any woman who receives forgiveness as a gift of love and then turns around and withholds it from others.

Do you want the cloud, the anchor, and the ball and chain, or do you want to start fresh today with a clean slate? It's up to you.

5

God Transforms Me

Christianity is coming to Christ as you are, receiving forgiveness and salvation, and then having the Holy Spirit create a new agenda for you and say, "I will enable you to pull it off."

SEVERAL YEARS AGO, at a conference in Mexico City, I met a best-selling author whose name you would recognize. I nearly fell over when he asked if I would join him for lunch and explain how he could become a Christian. As we ate and I began to explain it to him, he asked if I minded if he recorded it. "I would like to share it with my wife."

Twist my arm! Of course I complied, and then I carefully explained the big difference between religion and Christianity. Religion stresses what I can do to merit God's favor. What new leaf can I turn over? What new commitment can I make to get myself right with God?

Christianity says, "Admit you are a sinner and that *you* can't change that. Call out for a Savior who can do for you what you can't do for yourself: cleanse your past. Not only can He cleanse your sin, but He can also become your guide and your friend. He can energize your life and transform it."

I talked about a personal relationship with Christ. Throughout the conversation, he kept saying, "Yes, yes, I understand," as if to let me know he already knew all that. I was confused. Then the problem surfaced. He said, "I understand everything you just said, but I can't make a commitment to Jesus Christ. I'm the kind of a guy who always follows through on commitments. I know myself well enough to know that if I make a commitment to Jesus Christ, I won't be able to follow through with it. I will fail."

I cut in fast and wrote two words on a piece of paper. "Please don't ever use these two words— *commit* and *followthrough*—anymore," I said. "Becoming a Christian is not committing and following through. God *knows* you can't keep your commitment. God *knows* you can't follow through. Christianity is a matter of two different words: *receiving* and *trusting* God.

"Romans 6:23 says, 'For the wages of sin is death, but the free gift of God is eternal life in Christ Jesus our Lord.' What is a gift?"

He said, "Something you just receive."

"That's right. Salvation, regeneration, newness of life, forgiveness from sin are things that can only be received. And once you receive grace, once you receive forgiveness, you've got them. Your next step is to trust God and say, 'I don't know what all this means, and I don't know where I am going, but I am going to trust You each step of the way and see what happens."

That conversation took him off guard, by his own admission. When I saw him in the hallways between sessions of that conference, I would say, "Receive and trust."

He'd say, "I know. I'm thinking that over." Several months later he called my office and left a simple message with my secretary: "I received, and now I'm trusting!"

Harry and Jim

Many people considering Christianity are—just like my author friend—hesitant to take that final step across the line of faith because they are confused over the issue of transformation.

Let me illustrate this dilemma by telling you about someone we refer to at our church as Seeking Harry. He is an imaginary person, representing people we know who are somewhat interested in spiritual matters. He has a friend named Jim, another imaginary guy representing those in our church who want to reach out to the Harrys of our community. Jim is a devout Christian. He works in the same department as Harry does. Harry knows Jim is a Christian, because Jim leads a clean life—

squeaky clean. He is faithful to his wife, never uses profanity, and doesn't even know any shady jokes. Jim is kind and helpful and so honest he is almost sickening. Beyond that, Harry notices that Jim makes frequent references to his church, the little Bible study he is in, answered prayer, leadings from God, and so on.

Harry admires Jim more than he lets anybody know. If the truth were known, Harry's interest in spiritual matters is growing, due in part to Jim and in part to the process of elimination. Earlier in Harry's life he thought a college degree would satisfy him. Then he thought a good job would. Then a comfortable home became his goal. Then a wife, kids, Caribbean vacation, a promotion. But over time, he realized that achievements and acquisitions offered only temporary thrills. The satisfaction didn't last. Now, as he talks with and watches Jim, he gets the picture that Jim is running on different fuel.

There is sustained vitality in Jim's life. He seems connected to a positive life force that makes Harry more than a little envious. Harry would like to know more about Christianity. He would like to have what Jim has and find what his own soul is yearning for. But he just can't make the final move.

Harry keeps hanging back. He is stuck on third base. Do you know why? Because Harry can't picture himself being as gung-ho about Christianity as

Jim is. Harry is honest enough to say to himself, "I'll never be as squeaky clean as Jim is. I'll never be able to pray like Jim prays. I'll never like church as much as he does. As a child, I couldn't stand church."

Harry adds, "I hate Christian radio and television. I can't imagine myself in a Bible study. I don't even understand this Book, so why should I commit a Thursday night to studying it? I can't picture myself holding hands and singing 'Blest Be the Tie That Binds.' I can't imagine myself slapping another person on the back and calling him 'Brother.'"

Harry says, "No, I know myself too well. I can't change that much. I could never be a Christian like Jim. I could rev myself up for a short period, go through the motions, and fool people for an hour on Sunday. But sooner or later people would find out who I really am—Unholy Harry. So, why begin the charade? I won't be able to sustain it."

Woe Is Me

An illustration from nature further explains my point. Imagine you find a caterpillar that can talk. You overhear that fuzzy creature say, "I would love to become a brightly colored, high-flying butterfly, but all I can do is crawl around trying to look colorful. I've been trying to leap from branch to branch hoping to get the hang of flying. I am committed to becoming a butterfly, but it is hopeless. I am a brown, boring, branch-crawling caterpillar, and that's my destiny. Woe is me."

You'd be tempted to say to the caterpillar, "Look, friend, all the commitment in the world won't change you into a butterfly. But, if you cooperate with the miracle of metamorphosis, you can become a multi-colored, aeronautical phenomenon!"

Butterflies are really caterpillars who have been born again. In that sense they are just like you and me. God transforms us! He does something supernaturally in us and to us that we are utterly incapable of doing on our own. It's spiritual metamorphosis, God's transforming work in our lives.

If you're like our imaginary friend Harry, considering Christianity but hanging back because deep down you know you can't measure up to the standards, you know yourself well. What you need to understand is the old cart and the horse principle, spiritually speaking.

Most people think they have to change their ways, straighten out their lives, clean up their acts. They believe they have to *transform themselves* before they can become Christians. They try and fail, try again and fail again, try again and again and fail again and again. After a while, they stop trying. It's an exercise in futility.

The Bible says come as you are. Come in your sin. Come in your shame. Come in your weakness.

Come in your brokenness. Come in your failure. Romans 5:8 says that God directed His love toward you in that while you were still in the middle of your sin, Christ died for you. He offered you the gift of salvation, *while you were yet in your sin.*

Trust your life to Christ. Say, "Here it is. It's not much. It's full of sin and shame, remorse and failure. Here I am, a plain, old, branch-crawling caterpillar who has realized he can't change himself."

The Bible says that if we come to Christ as we are, He performs the miracle of salvation—that spiritual metamorphosis that infuses into our lives the power for total transformation. We come as we are; He makes us into that which we could never be apart from Him. Oh, please, understand the order of transformation. No more talk of committing and following through. It's a dead-end road.

Think rather of *coming* as you are and *receiving* grace. Receive forgiveness. Receive the gift of salvation and eternal life. Receive the Holy Spirit's power, and then trust God to bring about the transformation.

Are you a caterpillar tired of trying? Are you about ready to give it up? Are you weary of all the attempts over the years to transform yourself into a Christian? You can't do it. Stop trying. Come as you are. Let God do for you what you can't do for yourself.

The Process of Transformation

Let's say that you've come as you are and God has received you; by His grace He's given you the gift of salvation and newness of life. How does the process of transformation begin?

Simply put, once you are born again, it is the Holy Spirit's primary agenda, twenty-four hours a day, to bring about the total transformation. You will sense His presence. You will know it. There is no question about it. I am not talking about clouds parting and audible voices. I am talking about the unmistakable presence of a new form of energy that infuses your life with a power you never had before.

The Holy Spirit will use God's Word, the Bible, to stimulate new thoughts, new attitudes, a new agenda for your life. What was once an antiquated piece of literature will now be alive, vibrant, and relevant, transforming the way you think. As you read the Book or as you hear it taught, the Holy Spirit will say to your spirit, "This is truth. This isn't man's opinion. This isn't vain speculation. This is knowledge and wisdom that can be trusted."

God's Word will register with you as being profound, truly wise, and workable—something you need to act on in your life. At church or in a small group Bible study, something another believer says will ring true in your mind. You'll say, "This is amazing. This is what I need. This is the step I have to take. This is the wisdom I was looking for."

You will hear a song, and the Holy Spirit will confirm some truth in your mind. He'll say, "Let's not only hear this, but let's also heed it. Let's apply it."

The Holy Spirit will tug at your spirit and say, "It's time to grow in character," or "It's time to grow in relationships," or "It's time to change some misplaced values, to change your vocabulary, to change the way you handle your money, how you treat your body, how you treat your spouse and kids."

The miracle is that it is the Holy Spirit initiating the change. He is energizing you to make those changes. Friend, God's commandments are not burdensome. *Religion* places on your shoulders a long list of do's and don'ts. You find out real fast that you don't have the power to comply.

Christianity is coming to Christ as you are, receiving forgiveness and salvation, and then having the Holy Spirit create a new agenda for you and say, "I will enable you to pull it off."

Just Say Yes

You ask, "Do you mean I play no part in the transformation process? I sit in an armchair, feet up on the footstool and say, 'Transform me'?"

No. Your part is to do exactly what Galatians 5:25 tells you to do: "If we live by the Spirit, let us also walk by the Spirit." In other words, walk in the same direction the Holy Spirit leads you. I put it this way: Just say yes.

Say yes to the Holy Spirit. When He encourages you to make changes, He'll also enable and energize you. Your job is to cooperate.

Let me give you an example. Do you have a strained relationship with a loved one? If you are truly a believer, the Holy Spirit will tug at you to reconcile. You'll be tired of fighting. You'll want peace in that relationship. So if you say yes to the Spirit, you will take action to restore the relationship.

When He leads you in how you handle money, how you treat your body, how you establish your values, your part is to say, "I'll do it." That, my friend, is the pathway to transformation. It is God's initiative, God's energy, God's enabling power. Your part is to say yes. To cooperate.

Have you said no to the Spirit too often? The Bible says, "Don't quench the Holy Spirit" (1 Thessalonians 5:19). He wants to transform you into a spiritual butterfly, into someone with dignity, someone living the life designed for him by God. Right now in your spirit, say, "Lord, I want to stop bickering with the Holy Spirit and just say yes to every leading He gives me."

One Last Point

I have to warn you of something. You need to be aware of the extent of the transformation God has in mind for you. In *Mere Christianity* C.S. Lewis put it this way: "You must realize from the outset that the goal toward which He is beginning to guide your life is absolute perfection. No power in the universe except you, yourself, can prevent the Holy Spirit from taking you to that goal. We may be content to remain what we call ordinary, but the Holy Spirit is determined to carry out quite a different plan."

The goal of God's work in my life is complete and total transformation in every way possible. He wants to take this ordinary Dutchman and transform me into someone extraordinary in every way.

> Extraordinary in purity and love.
> Extraordinary in honesty and willingness to
>   admit mistakes.
> Extraordinary in concern for the poor.
> Extraordinary in concern over
>   discrimination.
> Extraordinary in how I treat my wife and
>   kids.
> Extraordinary in how I pastor.

God's plan for you is also extraordinary. Don't hang back. This is an adventure! Come as you are right now, and call upon the name of the Lord. Say, "I am asking You, Lord Jesus, to accept me. I receive, humbly, Your gift of grace, Your gift of salvation."

If you are not ready yet, then learn more, keep seeking, talk to friends, get your questions answered. But do it soon. Tomorrow may be too late.

6

God Guides Me

I need a guide who knows me, who understands me and has my best interests in mind. The best guide would understand my personality, my temperament, my gifts and abilities, my likes and dislikes. Wouldn't it be something to have a guide who takes all that into consideration as He charts a path for your life?

HOW WE COMPLICATE our lives! Aggressive types put down three-year goals, five-year goals, ten-year goals. We map everything out, create daily and weekly agendas, and write to-do lists—who to call, what to accomplish, deadlines to meet. We don't even offer our divine, capable, wise, caring Guide an opportunity to lead our lives. Some of us walk down dusty paths when we could be soaring under God's direction. Some of us twist ankles in the ruts of the road and would faint if anything supernatural happened.

The fact is that scores of Bible passages illustrate the fifth of the greatest wonders of the spiritual world—that our loving, trustworthy, forgiving, transforming God wants to guide our lives:

"I will instruct you and teach you in the way which you should go; I will counsel you with My eye upon you" (Psalm 32:8).

"And the Lord will continually guide you" (Isaiah 58:11).

"He guides me in the paths of righteousness" (Psalm 23:3).

"He will instruct him in the way he should choose" (Psalm 25:12).

"Trust in the Lord with all your heart, and do not lean on your own understanding. In all your ways acknowledge Him, and He will make your paths straight" (Proverbs 3:5–6).

To me, those promises are great news! The older I get the more I appreciate how confusing life can be. When I was in my late teens I had life all figured out. No complexities were beyond my comprehension. Now I realize how uncertain this world is, how limited my own experience is, how deceptive the evil one is, how easily I can be duped. I desperately need a guide through the maze of options every day. Don't you?

I need a guide who knows me, who understands me and has my best interests in mind. The best guide would understand my personality, my temperament, my gifts and abilities, my likes and dislikes. Wouldn't it be something to have a guide who takes all that into consideration as He charts a path for your life?

Such a guide exists, friend. God reaches out to you and says, in effect, "Take My hand. You matter to Me. I am trustworthy. I know you. I understand you. I know what will fulfill you. I created you."

Are you interested in that kind of guidance?

Are you at a crossroad in your job? Contemplating a career change? Maybe a transfer?

Do you face painful executive decisions that involve other people's futures? Do you face bankruptcy?

Your crossroad might be relational. Should you continue in this relationship? Where is it headed? Is it worth pursuing? Should you break up?

Do you face difficult days in your marriage? Are you considering marriage counseling? Are you separated? Should you reconcile?

Do you have strained relationships in your family?

Financial decisions, medical decisions, ministry decisions confront us all. I once faced three major decisions—as large as any I ever faced—all at the same time. I was at a crossroad. I was very glad I had a guide. A couple of those decisions had to be made by a certain time, and I honestly didn't know how it was all going to come out. But I knew I didn't have to worry. I was in His hands. He would guide me.

We receive divine guidance in four primary ways:

Through His Word

You may say, "Boring! I don't want a Bible study. I want a vision. I want a leaflet from heaven.

I want technicolor, 3-D, special effects. I want the clouds to part and an angel to visit me. I want it all."

People say they hear voices and see visions, and you say, "Here I stand at the crossroads, D-day is coming, and I don't get that stuff. What's wrong with me?"

God quietly responds, "I know what you want. I also know what you need. You don't need a vision. You don't need an audible voice. You need a Book. You need a road map. You need a blueprint. You need an instruction manual." Look for guidance in the Bible and you will find all you need for the rest of your life.

That's why the psalmist says, "Thy word is a lamp to my feet, and a light to my path" (Psalm 119:105). In effect, God says, "Do you need guidance about character matters, how to behave in this world, how to act? Do you need to know how to develop courage, integrity, and honesty? Do you need to develop patience, mature love, control anger? Look in the Book."

Do you need guidance to select a spouse? The Bible offers piercing insight into the kind of person with whom you should seek to build a permanent relationship. If you've already made a bad choice, the Bible offers instruction on how to turn it around and build a better marriage.

The wisdom in the Bible is wide and deep. No book offers better guidance about how to speak the truth in love, how to hold private peace talks, how to forgive one another, how to foster reconciliation rather than alienation.

Do you need to know how to handle money? Look in the Book. It talks about the danger of indebtedness. It talks about deceitfulness and greed.

Do you need guidance about how to conduct yourself in the marketplace?

How to manage people effectively?

How to receive direction properly?

How to work wholeheartedly within the range of who God made you to be?

How to raise children?

How to grow spiritually?

How to treat your body?

How to make your life worthwhile until you die?

How to go to heaven?

There is guidance in the Book.

Sometimes I wish the guidance in the Bible weren't so clear. It would be easier to say, "Well, you see, I just sort of lost my way. There was no road map and no blueprint. I got confused." If it weren't for the Bible, I could claim I was drowning in a sea of relativism. But the Book offers all the guidance a person needs to lead an effective, enjoyable, adventuresome, and worthwhile life. It contains clear instruction as to how to receive forgiveness in Christ and gain eternal life. No wonder

God encourages us to read it and listen to it when it is taught. We must study it, meditate on it, and heed it.

Do you take the Bible seriously? Do you read it? Do you seek to learn from it and to apply it so that its wisdom becomes operative in your life? When you hear it taught, do you take notes on ideas you want to retain and act on?

The Bible can keep you from destruction, but it has to be read and heeded. It has to be treasured. I make no apology for teaching from it every chance I get. I encourage our people to read it privately too.

Through Leadings from the Holy Spirit

This kind of guidance is miraculous. It is supernatural. It may make you feel uncomfortable—especially if you're a seeker who's not yet decided to trust Christ.

This second kind of guidance God offers is personalized guidance through leadings from the Holy Spirit. The Bible teaches that when we are converted, the Holy Spirit takes up permanent residence in our lives. One of His roles is to offer to every single believer specific, supernatural, highly personalized guidance. In the New Testament we read that the Holy Spirit led Peter, Paul, or Philip to go to this place or that, to say something, or to serve somebody. You may wonder whether that kind of leading from the Holy Spirit could work in your life. If you have not yielded your life and taken advantage of His leading, you don't know what you are missing. It is important to have the broad, generalized leadership and guidance that the Bible offers. But if you don't have that fine-tuned, direct, specific guidance system offered by the Holy Spirit, you are bypassing a major dimension of spiritual reality. This is the most exciting part of the Christian life!

Some people in our church wonder where I get my ideas for messages. Many times, during prayer, I put my feet up on my credenza, take a blank sheet of paper and say, "Lord, I'm just going to spend the next half hour or forty-five minutes listening to Your Holy Spirit. I am going to make myself available for His leadership." When the time is up, I usually have more than enough message ideas. It's amazing what can happen when we are yielded, humble, quiet before the Lord, and leadable.

Sometimes when I am getting those leadings from the Lord about what to speak on, I will also get other kinds of impressions. I'll be led to call someone who is under pressure. I might be nudged to serve him or give him something. I might be led to make a gift to the church or to do something special with my kids. These impressions the Holy Spirit makes on a yielded spirit and mind will open doors of opportunity and spiritual reality you never dreamed existed.

Vast numbers who call themselves Christians don't understand what I am talking about. They think their job as believers is to follow the rules. That's good, but there is more to Christianity than following rules. There is an adventure on which God wants to lead you.

When you go to work in the morning, you can simply do your job, or you can volunteer for a Spirit-led adventure. If I were going to the market-place on Monday morning, I would say, "Lord, I know I have a job to do. I have people to manage and deadlines to meet. But along the way, lead me. Show me a person to touch. Give me a new thought. Make an impression upon me as to how I can glorify You, how I can love others, serve my family and friends, serve employees and employers. Today I want to be leadable, so guide me by the hand of Your Holy Spirit."

When I am in tune with the Holy Spirit, it's not uncommon for me to be impressed to call someone. They will say, "I can't believe you called. I really needed to talk to someone just now." That's exciting.

Some time ago, Lynne and I were moved to give someone some money anonymously. Through the grapevine we heard that it came on the very day they needed it most. They glorified and praised

God for leading someone to meet their need. You can imagine how fulfilled we felt!

I don't know why so many people who claim to be Christians settle for a life of routine monotony when they could turn it into a Spirit-led adventure. The ruts of life are not attractive to me. But a daily adventure led by a supernatural Holy Spirit, that's where real life is!

You want a life like that? I challenge you to quiet your spirit every day, humble and yield yourself before the Lord, and seek His leadings. Then be prepared to make mid-course corrections throughout the day. Bring the Lord to mind and pray, "I'm still available. I'm still leadable. Are there any impressions You want to make on my spirit for me to do something, serve somebody, call someone, encourage somebody, share my faith with somebody? Just let me know."

Sometimes no impression will come. Other times a strong impression will surface. Follow it. A general rule is that if I follow the Holy Spirit's leadings, God sends more. If I quench those leadings, and say, "No, I know You want me to call somebody, but I'm not going to do it," I get fewer and fewer messages from God. It's as though God says, "I'll give you leadings that make life an adventure, but if you are not interested, go back to life in the ruts."

Are you yielded enough to receive these leadings? Are you interested? The apostle Paul calls it walking in the Spirit. Instead of carrying out your own priorities, say, "God, I want to be part of *Your* agenda today and every day."

The Holy Spirit will never lead you to do anything contrary to God's Book. His leadership and guidance are consistent and are to be measured against the standard of the Bible. Don't claim to have a leading to rob a bank, marry someone else's wife, or do something else destructive. *You* may want to rob a bank, but that is not God's leading. The Bible is the perfect way to test the validity of your leadings.

Through the Counsel of Godly Friends and Leaders

Proverbs 12:15 says, "The way of a fool is right in his own eyes, but a wise man is he who listens to counsel."

Proverbs 24:6 says: "In the abundance of counselors there is victory."

It hurts to learn of someone who made a tragic decision with devastating consequences, only to find that the whole fiasco could have been avoided. If that man or woman had had the humility, the maturity, the good sense to sit down with a seasoned, trusted believer and to say, "I'm facing a decision, and before I launch out on my own, I just want to know how you feel; give me counsel," peril probably could have been avoided.

Often God chooses to guide us through the counsel of others to remind us how intertwined we really are, that we are meant to live in community, that we are each other's keepers. If, in trying to make a major decision, I don't sense clear guidance from the Book or directly from the Spirit, I get a group of brothers and sisters together and tell them of my dilemma. So often, right in the middle of a conversation, the light goes on in my head and I wonder why I couldn't see the answer before.

I never make a major decision in my life, my marriage, my ministry, or my finances without sitting with trusted friends to hear their counsel. I have learned I am not all that smart. The world is more complicated than I thought when I was younger. The evil one is more scheming and deceptive than I gave him credit for. By subjecting myself to the wisdom of the Word, the leadings of the Holy Spirit, and to the counsel of godly men and women, I have spared myself, my family, and my congregation heartache.

Are you facing a decision that you should take to trusted friends? Don't be so arrogant as to believe God couldn't guide you through someone else's advice. God doesn't want us to be solo Christians.

He isn't asking you to run your life by parliamentary procedure, to gather a group and say,

"Okay, vote." He's merely asking you to consider their observations in your decision-making process.

Through Circumstances

Occasionally God gives us guidance by closing or opening a door of opportunity, but my counsel is to be very wary of your own motives in considering such things. Sometimes a young person wants to go to a certain school so badly that he believes God is leading him there, only to find out there are no openings. That should be accepted as a closed door.

On the other hand, even when some doors swing open wide, we must be careful not to naively attribute that to God. A man once told me, "I got a promotion and a $5,000 raise to move to a city down South. Now, it is going to wipe out my wife, and it's going to be very hard on our kids because they have roots here. This is the first church that we have really gotten deeply involved in, and we have grown spiritually. Our whole life and family has come together here. But the door is open, so we are moving."

Bad choice. More factors need to be considered than just open doors. The open door is possibly a small piece in the puzzle of determining what God would have us do. We have to go to the Word, to the Spirit, to our brothers and sisters in Christ. Be very careful about circumstances.

You say, "Sometimes when I need guidance, I don't get any from any source, and a decision has to be made. What do I do?"

Heed the words of Jesus, who said in Matthew 10:16, "Therefore be shrewd as serpents, and innocent as doves." When a decision has to be made and you have made yourself available, yet no specific direction comes, then use your sanctified common sense. He will honor your wisdom.

Fulfilled!

Friends, the wonder that God guides me often brings me to worship. While speaking at a college in New York, I mentioned almost in passing that many years ago I yielded my life to the Lord. I said that as I have continued to do this, I have been a very fulfilled man. I love what I am doing. I love where I am serving. After that message, a professor pulled me to the side and said, "You are the first Christian leader I ever heard say that kind of thing convincingly. I found myself believing you when you said that because God is guiding your life, you are a fulfilled man." Then he lowered his head. Neither of us said anything, but we both knew what was going on. He shifted uneasily as if to say, "I wish I could just let go and let God guide *my* life."

I looked at him as if to say, "I wish you could, too, because you don't know what you are missing."

Do you know what you're missing? Are you living beneath your privilege? Every day could be an adventure. God could be leading you by His Spirit through doors you never thought would open. He wants to guide your life. Will you let Him?

Will you read and heed the Word?

Will you be yielded and listen to and trust the leadings of the Holy Spirit?

Will you submit your plans to others for their input?

When you do, you'll find that life can truly be an adventure. And then you'll discover that God can use you.

7

God Uses Me

I guarantee that if you present yourself usable before the Lord, the Holy Spirit will lead and create opportunities for you. Then if you cooperate and do as He leads you, your light will shine in the darkness, your gloom will become like midday, and the Lord will satisfy your desire and give strength to your bones. You'll be like a watered garden, like a spring of water whose waters do not fail.

A COLLEGE ROOMMATE of mine lived with enormous anger because he had his legs blown up in Vietnam. He loaded up with pain pills, sat in a corner, sulked, and cursed. He said over and over, "I've been used. I was used."

Scores of people have felt the pain of being used in the business world. They say, "That company used me and then discarded me."

You know people who felt used in courtship or dating or even in marriage. They cry out with enormous emotion, "I was used!"

It can be awful to be used by someone.

On the other hand, strange as it may sound, it can be wonderful to be used by somebody. Quarterbacks hang around the coach, each hoping to be used. Each has that "I'm available" look. "Use me, coach."

Almost every week I meet with people after services who ask if I know anybody who could use a good salesperson or a hard-working bricklayer or a secretary. "I'd like to be used," they say.

We also have a steady stream of people who contact our church and say, "How can I be used around here? I'd love to be used."

As I write out my prayers early in the morning, almost every day I write, "Please God, please, use me today." From time to time God, in His grace, is pleased to use me in some way in someone's life. I cry out, "Thank You, Lord. I love being used by You."

Not much else in life compares to the thrill of being used by God to influence people or to advance God's purposes.

It is awful to be used by someone if you are deceived, manipulated, and taken advantage of by a self-seeking, self-centered person. But it is wonderful to be used if someone you respect, admire, and trust has a high-integrity endeavor that enthuses you. The God we've been talking about in this book —our loving, trustworthy, forgiving, transforming, guiding God—has endeavors in which He is more than willing to involve you. The first question is, do you know the Lord sufficiently? Do you love Him and respect Him and trust Him enough to believe that being used by Him is wonderful?

Separating the Men from the Boys

It's easy to determine whether someone really knows our Lord in a personal way, feels forgiven, and has the Holy Spirit working in his life. Just ask him if he wants to be a part of what God is doing. If a person is merely religious, or is just doing some spiritual window shopping, he'll respond, "Not particularly. I'm busy. I have important things to do." If you ask a true believer—one who has acknowledged his sinfulness before a holy God and trusted Christ for forgiveness—he'll say, "I'd be honored! That would be a privilege! When do I start?"

Some years ago I invited a friend to a ski trip to Colorado. He had never been skiing in the Rockies. He said, "No, I enjoy skiing right here in Southern Wisconsin at Wilmot Mountain." Every time he said "Wilmot Mountain," I said, "Whoa, time out here! Don't call that a mountain! Please!"

Finally, after the best sales job I could do, he relented and reluctantly joined me on that ski trip. As soon as we got out to Aspen, I took him directly to Aspen Mountain: 9,000 feet—jagged peaks, majestic pines, deep blue sky, eight inches of powder, two-mile ski runs. When we reached the top, he looked around and said, "I guess I didn't know what a mountain was."

I said, "I tried to tell you! You were content with that excuse for a mountain in Wisconsin while a real mountain, a majestic peak, was waiting for you!"

Isn't it frustrating to try to impress somebody who thinks a little molehill in the Midwest has anything to do with a majestic Rocky Mountain peak? That is what I'm wrestling with in this chapter.

So many just go along, spiritually window shopping, carefully excluding God from their agendas. They settle for so little! They ski on a molehill and call it big time! Sometimes I want to shout, "You don't know what you're missing!"

You don't really know what life is all about until you give your life to the Lord and receive salvation as a gift.

You receive cleansing and forgiveness.

You receive the power of the Holy Spirit.

You offer yourself to be used by God, and He uses you.

You feel the thrill of being used by God. You become part of something bigger than you.

You yield yourself to be used by God at work, in your family, in the neighborhood.

Hang On!

When you're on that path filled with serendipitous, supernatural workings of God, that's real life!

Some of us experience that regularly, and even while we feel the thrill of being used by God, the Holy Spirit whispers in our ears, "You ain't seen nothin' yet. I'm going to keep using you. This is going to be a ride!"

How I wish you could experience what I'm trying to describe. Once you've been to the Rockies, your perspective on Wisconsin skiing will change. And once you've been used by God, your perspective on your own agenda will change forever. That's why I had to include this miracle—God's eagerness to use us—in my list of the seven greatest wonders of the spiritual world. Let me describe just two of the countless ways God involves us in His eternal endeavors:

First, God uses people like you and like me to provide encouragement and assistance to the afflicted and oppressed of this world. In effect God says in Isaiah 61, "I want to use you people to bring good news to the afflicted, to bind up the brokenhearted, to proclaim liberty to captives, and freedom to prisoners . . . to comfort all who mourn." God wants to use us to feed the hungry, to bring the homeless into our homes, and to cover the naked.

One morning Lynne and I were at one of our favorite restaurants when an elderly waitress slipped and fell. The paramedics came and assisted her. Here she was, trying to maintain her dignity, probably very proud of herself that she could wait on tables and be self-supporting at her age. And now this. We both felt badly for her.

When Lynne and I went to bed that night she noticed I was quiet and asked if there was a problem. "I just can't get that woman out of my mind," I said. "I wonder if she's in a hospital. I wonder if she has family." We both wondered and worried.

But however tender Lynne or I were toward that woman was just a fraction of the concern that God has for anyone who's been a victim. We have no idea how God's heart breaks for those who are discriminated against or mistreated.

God's Executive Decision

I once went into a restaurant with a black member of our church. Everybody seemed to be looking. As we sat down, he said, "I get so tired of being a nigger. That's what people think I am. Everywhere I go, in every setting, every time I apply for a job, I'm black first, a man second."

No matter how badly I felt for him, I could hardly comprehend how deeply God feels for him. God cares about the poor and the homeless and the hungry and the discriminated against. He grieves for the handicapped, for the elderly, and for the infirm. We can't fathom how much God cares for people like that. In His Word He says that He could assign angels to care for those people, but He's made an executive decision. He wants to use us. He wants to involve us in convincing those people that they matter to Him. He says, "If you'll let Me use you to encourage and provide assistance to the afflicted and the oppressed, a new dignity will develop in you. You'll sense a personal integrity you didn't have before. You'll sense new self-worth, a new level of satisfaction. You'll finally realize, 'This is more in keeping with who I am!'"

In Isaiah 58:10, 11 God says that ". . . if you give yourself to the hungry, and satisfy the desire of the afflicted, then your light will rise in darkness, and your gloom will become like midday. And the Lord will continually guide you, and satisfy your desire in scorched places, and give strength to your bones; and you will be like a watered garden, and like a spring of water whose waters do not fail."

God is saying that if you will be usable, He will satisfy your soul. You will have a resurgence of spiritual power, emotional strength, and self-esteem.

I was running laps at the Y one November when a guy from our church jogged up next to me. "I had a fantastic Thanksgiving weekend," he said.

I said, "Oh? Where did you go?"

He said, "Some friends from church and I went downtown on Thanksgiving Day and served meals to vagrants on the street. It was fantastic. Best Thanksgiving I ever had."

The people who work in our church's food pantry, those who visit hospitals, those who work in our prison ministry, those who visit nursing homes, those who serve in substance abuse programs, do budget counseling, help with the benevolence board, they all know the truth of Jesus' words when He said, "It is more blessed to give than to receive" (Acts 20:35). What a thrill to be used by God to provide encouragement and assistance to the afflicted and the oppressed! You are always the greater winner.

But some continue to settle for less. Take a step and present yourself to our loving God and say, "Here I am. I'm available. Use me in any way You see fit. Use me to touch some forgotten person. Use me to encourage someone who is carrying a heavy load. Direct me to somebody I can encourage or assist."

No Greater Thrill

I guarantee that if you present yourself usable before the Lord, the Holy Spirit will lead and create opportunities for you. Then if you cooperate and do as He leads you, your light will shine in the darkness, your gloom will become like midday, and the Lord will satisfy your desire and give strength to your bones. You'll be like a watered garden, like a spring of water whose waters do not fail.

God also uses people to announce that moral failures matter to God. Jesus traveled throughout Palestine and showed people that even though they were caught in adultery and miserably failed God's moral standards, they still mattered. Though there were swindlers, liars, thieves, rich, poor, black, white, male, female, young, old, educated, uneducated, Jesus just kept saying, "You matter to me, and I offer you new life."

Jesus died for the sins of the world, and He was resurrected in power, proving His deity. As He was about to ascend to the Father, having completed His task, He turned to His ragged band of followers and said (paraphrasing from Acts 1), "Do you want a challenge that will bring meaning and purpose to your life? Let Me use you to spread the word all over the world that all people—even moral failures —matter to God. You will be my witnesses. I could drop leaflets from heaven, I could assign angels, but no. I want to involve you to be My ambassadors. The Holy Spirit will give you courage and energy and wisdom and anything else you need."

The Book of Acts tells us the disciples took the challenge and that they turned the world upside down. They got the word out, and they experienced the thrill of being used by God to inform people of the greatest news of all.

From the Bible and from church history we know that Jesus' followers suffered physical beatings and persecution, were imprisoned, fed to lions, burned at the stake, even sawn in half. Yet until they died, they kept spreading the word.

That amazes me, but it shouldn't. If you've ever informed somebody that they matter to God, and if that person listened and understood and repented and received Christ and started to grow, you know the thrill of seeing somebody's life and eternity affected because God used you. You! Tell me what beats that! What gives a human being a greater sense of purpose and fulfillment than knowing that God used him? Occasionally I hear from someone, "God used you to lead me to Christ, and so my life and my future was changed." God in His love allowed me the privilege of being His ambassador.

Is it time you accepted that privilege and said, "I want to be used to encourage and assist the afflicted and oppressed, and I want to be used to inform the world that sinners matter to God, that their forgiveness is available through Christ"?

There are things to be feared more than death:

A wasted life.

A life unattached to God's great endeavors.

A self-willed, self-absorbed existence, narrow and routine and ultimately unsatisfying.

A life wasted fooling around in the foothills of Wisconsin when majestic peaks await you in Colorado.

Just pray: "I'm available, God. Please use me."

8

God Satisfies Me

Satisfaction begins when you discover that you matter to God and that God can be trusted. Satisfaction continues as you experience over and over the forgiving power of God. Then God initiates and enables the transformation process in your life. . . .

"Phil has not found himself yet."

"Jill is getting restless."

"Tom bought a bigger boat, honey."

"Jane is applying for another transfer."

"Mark is having a pre-midlife crisis."

"Max is having a midlife crisis."

"Marv is having a post-midlife crisis."

"Bob is bored with life."

"Tim thinks his vacation will turn his life around."

"Don is going back to school for another degree."

"David is dreaming of taking early retirement and opening a bed and breakfast place. He's thirty-six years old."

"Lori will be OK once she gets married."

Recognize the theme? Can you hear all the

"if only's" in those bits of conversation? "Some day, some way, sometime, somewhere, somehow, I'll manage to satisfy myself. Just give me a few more days or weeks or months or years, a few more breaks. Let me win the lottery."

On and on goes the myth that people can satisfy themselves. Capitalism flourishes on this myth.

Afflicted with Affluence

On the authority of the Word of God, I say this: No people can experience ultimate satisfaction apart from the miraculous activity of God in their lives. Oh, how people have tried! And oh, how they have failed! Throughout history, people have attempted to satisfy themselves through the amassing of fortunes, only to learn to their utter consternation that Ecclesiastes 5:10 is as true today as it was when it was written thousands of years ago: "He who loves money will not be satisfied with money, nor he who loves abundance with its income. This too is vanity."

Have you ever noticed that great wealth is often accompanied by a poverty of spirit and an absence of joy? Some of the neediest people I know are afflicted with affluence. Occasionally someone will try to impress me with his or her wealth, but I can usually see through it. At the end of a conversation these people usually say, "But there are just a few matters I'd like to talk to you about . . . ."

If I feel the right kind of rapport with them, I say, "Do you want to talk about your affliction with affluence?"

I understand that kind of thing. Many of the affluent have envisioned a fairy tale existence—complete with large American homes, expensive Italian wardrobes, German cars, French food, and South African jewelry. They think if they could ever get close to that lifestyle, they would be ultimately, profoundly, and continually satisfied. But when some measure of affluence comes, it doesn't turn out at all as they thought.

Don't misunderstand; earning money can be challenging and interesting and exciting, and there doesn't have to be anything wrong with it. But sooner or later you find that amassing wealth doesn't offer ultimate inner satisfaction.

A friend once told me, "When I was a kid, I told myself that if I ever made $15,000 a year, I would be happy. Then in my thirties, I said if I could ever make $50,000 a year, I would be content. In my forties, I said if I could ever earn $80,000 a year, I would be content. Well, I make a six-figure income now, and I am greedier than I have ever been."

How about the car that was going to be the answer to everything? Someone in a parking lot bangs the door, and that's the end of that thrill. No matter what we think will satisfy us, once we have it a while, we know: that wasn't it.

The First Century Yuppie

Some people attempt to satisfy themselves by pursuing pleasure: travel, food, sports, sex, drugs.

Honest pleasure seekers eventually find what the writer of Ecclesiastes meant when he said that seeking pleasure is like chasing the wind. *The Living Bible* puts it this way: "Anything I wanted, I took, and did not restrain myself from any joy. I even found great pleasure in hard work. This pleasure was, indeed, my only reward for all my labors. But as I looked at everything I had tried, it was all so useless, a chasing of the wind, and there was nothing really worthwhile anywhere" (Ecclesiastes 2:10–11).

One of the most vivid illustrations of this is the conversation Jesus had with a first century yuppie, traditionally referred to as the rich young ruler (recorded in Matthew, Mark, and Luke). In today's language, this man is young, upwardly mobile, and professional. He is a highly educated investment banker, stock broker, commodities trader, computer wizard, or entrepreneur. He drives a BMW with dark side windows and a sound system that can shatter those windows. He is well-dressed, in excellent shape, and walks with confidence. In most people's eyes, he has it all. He's a walking commercial for the good life.

But watch where he's walking. He's heading to a private conversation with a renowned Bible teacher. He checks to make sure no one is looking, then says quietly with a hint of embarrassment, "I don't really have it all. People think I do. I thought I did. But I don't. I am not satisfied."

The Bible teacher says, "You aren't satisfied?"

The young man says, "Shh! For pete's sake, can you keep it between us? I have worked hard. I have handled every challenge I have been faced with. I've overcome obstacles, found ways to win the games of life, and I have the toys and symbols to prove it; but I can't figure out how to satisfy myself. I can't do that one thing."

You can read the rest of the account in the Scriptures, but what fascinates me is that the man who has everything realizes he doesn't have enough. That's a paradox, isn't it? The man who has been able to amass money, experience pleasure, and achieve success can't satisfy himself.

The answer to his dilemma is profound: God satisfies. He does things for us and in us that we can't do for ourselves.

God meets inner needs.

He quiets restlessness and turmoil.

He ministers to longings.

He soothes wounds.

He calms fears.

He satisfies our souls.

Psalm 103:5 says that God ". . . satisfies your years with good things, So that your youth is renewed like the eagle."

What do eagles do? They soar. The psalmist is saying that God promises He will satisfy our souls so completely that our inner spirits will soar! God says, "You can't make your spirits soar, but I can, and I will if you let Me."

In Psalm 23:5, the psalmist talks about being so satisfied that he feels his cup is running over. He's about to burst with satisfaction. God is saying, "You cannot fill your own cup with money, with pleasure, or with status. But, *I* can fill your cup until you feel you are bursting."

How Does God Satisfy Our Souls?

Let's go back to the first great wonder of the spiritual world. God loves me. Do you know any love-starved person who claims to be satisfied? I have never met one. Love-starved people go from friend to friend and lover to lover and spouse to spouse and therapist to therapist. They will never be satisfied until they are loved with a perfect and everlasting love. Ultimate satisfaction in the soul begins with the knowledge that God treasures you, that you are the object of God's affections, that He thinks about you day and night, that He listens to you, that you are precious to Him. And when you understand and accept that you matter to God, you heave a sigh of relief and say, "I may not matter much to the butcher, the baker, or the candlestick maker, but I matter to God. He treasures me and He loves me."

It Ain't the Cake

Earlier in my life, I was idealistic. I thought human love could satisfy me. Finding the right mate, I thought, would meet my love need. I have a wonderful mate, but she doesn't satisfy my inner love need.

You may be thinking, *All I need is a marriage partner, and then my love need will be met.* It's not going to be enough. You have to come to grips with the fact that only the purity and the depth and breadth and height of God's love for you will ever satisfy.

I thought if I got a group of close friends, that would do it. God's given me more friends than I deserve, and they love me. It's wonderful, but it doesn't meet my inner love need.

The love of my wife and kids and the love of my friends and co-workers is like frosting on the cake, but it ain't the cake. Satisfaction begins when we discover that we matter to God. Beyond that, as we discover that the God who loves us can be trusted, satisfaction, peace, and inner contentment will grow. Over time, we learn that God will keep His promises, because of His great love, and out of that love will come the reality that He proves

Himself over and over to be an absolutely trustworthy God and friend.

When God promises that He will never leave us or forsake us, He can be trusted. When He says He will grant us strength for the storms of life, we'll find He can be trusted during the worst of storms! When He says His wisdom will lead us on the best path for life, He can be trusted. Over time, our satisfaction deepens as our loving God proves Himself trustworthy.

Have you ever met a shame-filled person who claimed to lead a satisfied life? How satisfied could he feel? Do your spirits soar when you fail God, or your spouse, or your employer, employee, kids, or parents? How about when you're filled with remorse and feel that awful self-reproach and self-hatred as you cower in fear of punishment?

Psychologists tell us that one of the driving forces behind spending sprees is guilt. When somebody is down on himself, he believes the television commercials that say, "Go out to dinner, go to a movie, buy a new suit. You'll feel better!"

But you will never experience ultimate inner satisfaction if you remain filled with shame. The answer? God forgives failures. Lovingly, thoroughly, no matter how serious or embarrassing they are, God forgives us on the basis of what Jesus did on the cross. When He died for us and absorbed our punishment, not only did God forgive our failures, but the Holy Spirit also removed the guilt, the self-reproach, and the fear of punishment. He paved the way for the return of satisfaction in our spirits.

Satisfaction begins when you discover that you matter to God and that God can be trusted. Satisfaction continues as you experience over and over the forgiving power of God. Then God initiates and enables the transformation process in your life.

Static people are never satisfied people. God created human beings in His image. We are created to be dynamic, to grow, to flourish, to take risks, to develop, to stretch ourselves, to feel the challenge of achievement and accomplishment. We will only be ultimately satisfied if we are growing, progressing, and changing for the better in relationships, in character, in talents, and in the development of our abilities. Bored people, people who are stuck, people who vegetate are never ultimately satisfied. God knows that, so He puts the Holy Spirit in our lives and says, "I will point out the changes you need to make. I will energize you, give you the desire and the ability to grow and flourish. All you need to do is cooperate and walk in the Spirit." Say yes to the Holy Spirit and you will feel yourself growing.

It Feels Great to Grow

When the elders tell me they've seen growth in certain areas of my pastoring or preaching, I think of a dozen times I have failed in those very areas. But it is music to my ears to hear that they see growth in my life. It feels great to grow! It is satisfying to have someone say, "You're more patient than you used to be. You're kinder than you used to be. You're more honest than you used to be. You display more discipline and courage than you used to."

God says, "I want you to grow, and I will assume the responsibility to transform your life. Just cooperate with Me."

Outrageous Grace

No one whose life is spinning in circles can claim to lead a satisfied life. People tell me, "My life is going nowhere. I sense no direction, and it frustrates me."

I say, "I'm sure it does. But God has custom designed you. He knows your personality and temperament. He knows your talents, gifts, and abilities. He knows what you like and dislike. He knows what will fulfill you. He says, 'Let Me guide your life. I will get it on a path that has purpose and direction and meaning.'"

To top it all off, our loving, trustworthy, forgiving, transforming, guiding God is so outrageously gracious that He involves us, uses us, gets us to participate with Him in His plans to change the world. God dignifies us by entrusting to us the enormously important mission of influencing our world for Christ and for eternity.

He uses us as His emissaries to encourage and assist afflicted people. He uses us to inform everybody everywhere that they matter to God. It is wonderfully satisfying to be used by God to touch human life.

It All Fits Together

If a man or woman is loved with a perfect love by a God who is absolutely trustworthy, One who can and will completely forgive the past, who initiates exciting transformations, who offers personalized guidance down the best path, who then uses that man or woman in supernatural ways to affect other people, you tell me: will that man, will that woman lead a satisfying life? Yes, even if all the external circumstances aren't ideal, even if that man or woman can't afford a microwave or a VCR!

Ultimate satisfaction is the result of being rightly related to God through Christ and then yielded to God's transforming, guiding, and enabling work. God wants your spirit to soar. He wants your cup to overflow. He wants to satisfy your soul. You're not going to find satisfaction by amassing fortunes, pursuing pleasures, or achieving status. Only God can satisfy your soul.

You say, "I believe you in a spiritual sense, but I

still have some basic necessities, some external needs. Does God care about a house, a car, a job, a spouse?"

Yes, He does. David, the giant killer, was abundantly blessed, satisfied in his soul. God had been gracious to him, but David had a problem. Though God had satisfied him internally and had satisfied almost all his external needs, David wanted more. He took matters into his own hands and claimed another man's wife. He lusted after a woman and had to have her. You know the story.

David was confronted by a prophet named Nathan, and through him God spoke to David about satisfaction. God says, "It is I who anointed you King over Israel. I put you on the throne. I delivered you from the hand of Saul. I put you in the palace. I gave you the House of Israel and Judah to rule over. And if that had been too little, I would have added many more things like these to you."

God promises, "I'll satisfy your external needs too." Psalm 84:11 says: "No good thing does He withhold from those who walk uprightly."

You can be satisfied today. You can look at the externals you don't have and be discontented and dissatisfied, or you can change the channel of your mind and say, "God loves me, and that loving God can be trusted! He forgives my failures! He's transforming me! He's guiding me! He's using me! He satisfies me! I am of all men, of all women, most blessed. Thanks be to God."

9

Now What?

God can do amazing things through His people. He said He would build His church and the gates of hell would not prevail against it. Gates are defensive. We, His people, are to be on the offensive.

PERHAPS YOU'RE NOW AWARE of the seven greatest wonders of the spiritual world for the first time. You're resting in God's love, satisfied that He can be trusted, grateful that He forgives you, excited that He will transform you, eager to have Him guide you and use you and satisfy you.

Now what do you do?

The apostle Paul, whose first century letters to Christians make up most of the New Testament, encouraged believers to grow in their individual relationships, to band together in the name of Christ, to form churches and not "forsake the assembling" of themselves together.

Study Paul's letter to the Romans and you'll discover some of the characteristics he thought should epitomize such churches. As a believer, new or old, you'll want to be sure to attend a church characterized by the following:

In every true church there must be a *pastor* devoted to Jesus Christ, yielded to the Holy Spirit, gifted, and dedicated to using his gifts to lead and feed the flock. Rarely will you see a flourishing church without an authentic, gifted, yielded, usable pastor.

Secondly, surrounding that pastor must be a group of *church leaders* who, with the pastor, guard the vision of the church and keep the believers and the pastor on track. When the apostle Paul appointed a pastor in a church he was leaving, he assigned the pastor and the other believers the task of calling a group of godly elders.

Thirdly, every solid church has to have *point people*—men and women God calls and equips to lead various ministries within the body.

Beyond that, there must be *pillar people*—men and women who love Christ and the church so much they are willing to serve as soldiers in the various areas in which they have been called and gifted. A great pastor, wonderful elders, and fantastic point people are worthless without pillar people who surround them and say, "Put some of the load of ministry on my shoulders. I'll carry it. I'll serve faithfully. I'll pay the price. I'll die to myself. I'll even die literally, if need be."

Further, every successful church needs *potential pillar people,* believers in training, those discovering their spiritual gifts and preparing to become pillar people. They may be recuperating from wounds, putting their lives back together, recovering from lives ravaged by sin. They are tomorrow's pillar people, ready in due season.

In every church a group exists that would have bothered the apostle Paul. I call them the *promiscuous people*—not necessarily sexually promiscuous, but including that. More specifically, these people call themselves Christians but prefer comfort, pleasure, convenience, and spectating over discipleship, devotion, servanthood, and soldiering for the cause of Christ.

The promiscuous people destroy the morale of the body. The apostle John called them lukewarm, making God sick because they were neither hot nor cold.

Periodically I make a point of serving notice on the promiscuous people in our church. I say, "If I were a promiscuous person, I'd repent of apathy and half-heartedness or find another church. It's going to be very uncomfortable around here in the coming months. Your pastor, your elders, the point people, the pillar people, and the potential pillar people are planning the next offensive assault into enemy territory. We are eager to advance the cause of Christ at any cost. Please take the time to ponder what you are doing with your one and only life."

Why? Partly because Christ calls us to His soldiering service. But also, think about it: what else is there to do with our lives? What else in this world is of any consequence?

Now that you are responsible for your knowledge of the seven greatest wonders of God's spiritual world, what will you do? Where will you stand? Will you join a church as described above, or will you be a promiscuous person, squandering time in the barracks while the soldiers are on the front lines? Make a decision. The Word of God and the Holy Spirit will press in on you, and you'll find lukewarmness uncomfortable.

If you are an *elder,* a servant, a soldier, God bless you. Keep serving Him.

If you are a *point person,* courageous, visionary, and dedicated to the advancing of the cause of Christ, God bless you. Be encouraged. Be strong.

If you are a *pillar person,* your commitment deserves biblical recognition. God bless you for serving selflessly and soldierlike.

If you are a *potential pillar person,* in training, recuperating, readying yourself for pillar person duty, your day is coming. Lay a firm foundation. Ready yourself so you can serve as a soldier for the rest of your life. God bless you.

God can do amazing things through His people.

He said He would build His church and the gates of hell would not prevail against it. Gates are defensive. *We,* His people, are to be on the offensive.

So seek first His kingdom. Don't get entangled. Don't get choked out. Don't lose your first love of the Lord. Don't lead a lukewarm life. Be a pillar person, a servant, a soldier.

I'm embarrassed at how many times I've been promiscuous, in the sense that often I've tried to be a Christian without being willing to bear a cross. I've preferred comfort. I've tried to find a pain-free way of following Christ.

I need to learn more about dying. I need to learn more about soldiering. Perhaps you can say the same. Pray that God will make you clear-minded, that He will convince you there's nothing else in life as meaningful, as significant, as exciting, as challenging as trying to reach a lost, crazy, mixed-up world with the only hope in the universe —the saving message of Jesus Christ.

May you be a soldier in a church that is like a city on a hill, a lighthouse, salt and light, a land-mark, a hospital, a launching pad, a training center, a family.

May you glorify God in every way you can. And when you stand before God someday, may you hear, "Well done, good and faithful servant, faithful soldier, pillar person, support column in the most important work in the world."

ABOUT THE AUTHOR

Bill Hybels is founder and pastor of Willow Creek Community Church in S. Barrington, Illinois, one of the fastest growing churches in the U.S. He is also the author of *Who You Are When No One's Looking, Laws That Liberate, Christians in the Marketplace,* and *Caution: Christians Under Construction.*